We were meant

to shine !

Orien Bouk

© 2015 In Your Own Words 2015 by Onlee Bowden.

For information contact;
In Your Own Words
221 Garland Street
Traverse City, Michigan 49684
htp://www.flipitonitsear.com

ISBN: 978-0-9963629-9-3
First Edition: May 2015

10 9 8 7 6 5 4 3 2 1

Dedication

With much gratitude, I dedicate this book to the following individuals:
To my early mentors Dr. Janet Yerby and Dr. Albert Lewis for providing an exciting
platform for discovery as well as a soft cushion to land on when needed.

To the department of Speech Communication and Performing Arts of Central Michigan University for framing my understanding of communication and for allowing me
to be part of an exceptional team of educators.

To Kris Stableford, Dr. Shelly (pig dog sister) Hinck, and Dr. Gail (oh baby, oh baby)
Mason for being my communication nerds and fellow
all-things-irreverent aficionados.

To Mom and Dad for leaving behind a treasure-house of great and worthy stories that
are now fondly etched into perpetuity.

To my daughter Angie and my oldest grandson Taylor for being thoughtful, open, and
funny in their ways and to all of my grandchildren for staring in so many
of my favorite stories.

To my family and friends from Haiti for teaching me so much about the authentic
voice. Thank you for shaping me in unexpected and amazing ways.

To my sweetie-pie husband Lee for seeing me through this project with more humor
than not. Can't wait to be a road gypsy with you by my side!

Finally, I dedicate this book to my clients who have trusted the process and me
enough to give new ways of speaking a fair shot. I love watching your transformation
from uncertainty and anxiety to calm confidence. Thank you for allowing me to help
you do this, and thank you for keeping me honest in my work.

Contents

Part 1 : Revealing the Mystery behind Public Speaking

Part 2 :You on Skills, or How to Become an Effective Speaker

Preface

My Favorite Speakers

When Ordinary spends time with her good friends Ability and Grace,
she feels quite extraordinary indeed!

- Onlee Bowden

People who ask me to list my favorite speakers are usually surprised at how I respond. The fact is, I expect professional speakers to be good. After all, they're professionals. I don't expect famous people to be good, but if they are, that's great. Famous people are famous for a reason, and that's the draw in listening to them.

Instead, I'm most impressed by everyday people who speak because they know they will regret it if the moment passes by. My daughter Angie comes to mind. About four years ago, my mother passed away. My daughter asked to say a few words at her funeral. She wrote out what was in her heart and spoke with all the love she felt. My heart exploded as I listened to her carefully chosen words. Here is what my daughter said:

Before I lead us in prayer, I would like to share a few thoughts.

Today you will hear the stories of my grandmother's life. Some of these include her experiences as a girl, then a young woman, a wife, a mother, and finally a grandmother, but for a few minutes, I would like to share with you the moment my grandmother passed away.

During the time we waited for her strong-willed body to finally lay itself to rest, there was always a family member holding and kissing her hands, running their fingers through her hair, or fussing over whether she was comfy enough.

The beautiful part is that all of her children were there telling childhood stories, laughing, weeping, and supporting each other through their time of need.

I read a saying once, that "Friends are God's apology for family." This may be true at times, but it sure wasn't the case here. I can say one thing for this family…When tragedy strikes, we all unite for comfort and a loving shoulder to cry on. I sure hope that when I pass, my boys show me the honor Grandma's children have given her.

Through all of this, there is one special person I really want to capture…my Uncle Stanley.

Stanley never left his mother's side. We even had a hard time convincing him that it was all right to please go and brush his teeth! He stood next to her side, frequently letting her know that she was loved, a wonderful mother, and that we were all there with her. When her moment came, he was the only one with her, and it warms my heart to the core to know that he wasn't robbed of that very special moment. My Aunt Jane said it so true: "We know Mom was waiting for her and Stanley to be alone, because that's the way she would have wanted it."

Grandma, as your grandchild, I will miss your sugar-coated pancakes and snuggles wrapped up in a towel after a bath when you would rock me, singing, "I love you a bushel and a peck." And now I can even say I will miss the "huge" handmade underwear you always sewed for us as children.

After everything is said and done, I sure hope there was a huge Mardi Gras parade waiting for your grand arrival into heaven...You bet your dirty neck I do.

We never know when or where we will be called to speak. It's never about being perfect; it's just about being real. That's why my favorite speakers are regular people who have learned to speak with their feet solidly on the ground and their hearts wide open.

I love to listen to Tony Anderson, Steve Merten, and Fran Martin share their stories. These folks are so gut real. I love listening to Patty Cantrell because she beautifully conveys her message in a down-to-earth rhythm that leaves her audience rocked. I love watching my brother Stan when he speaks; he's humble yet risky. He's not at all afraid of using great attention getters and cleverly weaving them into his presentation. He's so dialed in he can get himself out of any corner, even better than I can.

I love listening to Victoria Hughes. After she brings the house down with some audaciously beautiful song, she shares what's in her heart, and I'm mesmerized. I bow to my Haitian friends Mitou, Ephraim, Naomi, Claude, and Jephthe, who translate for me.

Perhaps you're thinking to yourself, "I'm not the kind of speaker you're talking about. I have to present updates to upper management, not belt out a song or a message of faith."

No matter; it works just the same. My brother is a school superintendent, and before that, a community foundation director. Steve Merten owns an insurance agency. Tony Anderson is the general manager of a local electric company. The majority of my clients are bankers, engineers, business owners, executives, and managers. I have clients who've incorporated public speaking into their professional development plans for all their employees. No matter the job title, all speakers have the same basic desire: to sound real and have something to say.

That's really all you have to do. When this happens, your speaking is effective. Believe me when I say that you can become one of these individuals. When you convey not only your words but also your passion, you will take your audience on a journey that crosses cultures.

Go ahead. Flip public speaking on its ear. Embrace the approach I present in *Flip It on Its Ear, a Radical Approach to Public Speaking*. Sound real and have something to say. You'll never regret doing so.

Introduction:

It's a New Age

Outdated knew she was old-fashioned, but she was afraid.
Then one day Change took her to the ocean.
- Onlee Bowden

I remember taking my first public speaking class in 1973. We used note cards, wrote out every word of every speech, and were graded on how many "ums" we used. When we finished, we were given a long list of what we'd done wrong as our classmates looked on.

I received a solid C+.

Ironically, while today's public speaking classes often mirror this dated approach, the people taking them are vastly changed.

We are a cross-generation of global citizens, breaking down barriers at every turn. Access to information is transforming our opportunities to think, create, and share. Most importantly, our expectations for authenticity in communication have never been higher. Our audience is now global, and our communication technologies continue to emerge at warp speed, connecting us to one another in increasingly personal ways.

The voice of the citizen is more influential than at any former time in history. With the touch of a finger, we, the citizenry, can shape public opinion.

What this means is that real communication skills have never been more in demand than they are right now. At the height of the most recent economic downturn, community colleges were bursting at the seams. The world is demanding more fluid and agile people, and individuals realize they need to step it up if they want to remain in the game. Skills such as leadership, creative thinking, and the ability to speak in front of others are reshaping the landscape. We must be able to share information at a moment's notice, but – and here's the catch – in an authentic way.

What's more, almost every time we speak to another person, we are involved in some form of public speaking. This includes answering the telephone, presenting to colleagues, and participating in conference calls and webinars. It certainly isn't limited to formal speeches.

This book offers a new approach to public speaking. It makes the claim that everyone has the right to experience freedom through the spoken word. It embraces the introvert and the extravert with equal respect. It stands solidly in the belief that readers already possess the most important elements for speaking inside themselves. It strips away the mystery surrounding public speaking and replaces it with clear direction.

More specifically, Flip It on Its Ear offers a new and vastly improved method of writing notes and preparing to give a speech, including tips for dealing with nerves and tips to improve your ability to speak in conference calls, meetings, and other public-speaking environments. It also includes advice on using stories plus the nuts and bolts of putting it all together. In short, this two-part book offers a new approach that creates long-term positive change.

My personal wish for every reader, every speechmaker, and every would-be speechmaker is that you find a new sense of inspiration and confidence in yourself as a sharer of thoughts and ideas. I want you to tell your story, share your point of view, and speak for those who cannot. Having refused to let fear get in your way, I want you to be free of regrets later in life.

I wrote Flip It on Its Ear to get you off the mark and moving forward, so join the conversation, say what's on your mind, and share the vision, in your own words.

Part One:

Revealing the Mystery behind Public Speaking

Mystery is so good at hide-and-go-seek that one time she fell asleep and no one missed her.
- Onlee Bowden

A mystery surrounds public speaking, something almost elusive. We fear public speaking, yet somehow we are drawn to it. Like snakes, spiders, or sharks, it triggers undeniably strong emotions. We watch others and wonder, "How do they do that? What do they know that I don't? Why are they unafraid while I tremble? Why can't I be a good public speaker?"

I want you to know that you can be a good public speaker. If you take the time up front to understand the inner workings behind public speaking, you can achieve a deep and lasting transformation.

Unfortunately, many individuals are looking for the short list, the easy answer to public speaking. Clients call and say, "I just need to get through this upcoming event; I don't need to become a real public speaker."

Sometimes I can help them, but generally it's not that easy. There simply isn't a quick fix to standing in front of others feeling calm and organized. Most of my clients have somewhere between two and five decades of ingrained and inconsistent public speaking habits. Inconsistent strategies result in inconsistent results, and that truly is not something anyone can relax with.

Part One of Flip It on Its Ear peels back the "you" in public speaking by exploring the psychology behind performance, fear, the critical voice, and concentration. It is written to offer a new perspective on public speaking by revealing how we think and operate as speakers.

As a teacher, I've learned that when there is a balanced mix of the "why" behind skill sets, clients make faster and longer lasting change. Consequently, this section is fashioned to begin the process of understanding public speaking on a deeper level.

After examining the psychology of fear and the myth of perfection, I introduce a philosophy that underlies communication and its impact on speaking. Finally, the last chapter in this section considers the impact of public speaking in the business world.

Chapter One:

Fear and All Its Partners in Crime

Guard yourself from Judgment; he is Fear's best friend. Judgment plays
a mean game of checkers and usually always cheats to win. He loves to
shout, "King Me!"

- Onlee Bowden

C onsider this: the right to speak is protected by the U.S.
Constitution, yet the number one fear in the United States
continues to be public speaking.

Why is fear so prevalent? What is it about public speaking
that creates such a visceral feeling of terror in so many intelligent
and motivated individuals?

It could be argued that our fear of public speaking is, in part,
attached to our culture and, further, that it dates back to the
Church of England and our Puritan beginnings. In addition to
their appetite for freedom and a hardy work ethic, the Puritans
firmly believed that children were to be seen and not heard. Seen
and not heard.

1

At first glance this may not seem like a big deal, but those who have delved into the psychology of fear will argue that individuals who are encouraged to share stories when they are children are more comfortable speaking in public when they become adults.

My friend Marguerite is a great example. Marguerite is second in command at our local college and speaks regularly in public. She also happens to be one of the best speakers I know at the non-pro level. I thoroughly believe good speakers are not born but rather are molded by their environments, so I was interested in her back story. Over drinks one evening, I asked her about it.

She told me that as a little girl growing up in her home country in Latin America, Sundays were special. Everyone gathered around a large table loaded with familiar dishes. When the feasting was done, cigars were lit, wine was poured, and the stories began. Everyone had a story, beginning with her grandpa, moving to her uncles and aunties, and concluding with the children. When it was her turn, her grandfather would turn to her and say, "Marguerite, tell us a story." While she spoke, everyone listened, encouraged, exclaimed, and asked questions.

At that, I got it. As a child, Marguerite had learned that her voice was worthy of attention. By being encouraged to elaborate, she learned to expound on her stories and add texture. She learned how to speak in a safe and supportive environment, which allowed her to develop a deep sense of ease in front of others.

How many of us had that sort of experience as children? Only a few, more than likely. Our culture continues to be more interested in the stories of adults than children. We are overworked, usually underpaid, and trying to juggle too many responsibilities to ask ourselves if we are encouraging "voice worthiness" in our children. Thus, the majority of us don't learn to speak comfortably in front of others at an early age, and we carry our feelings of inadequacy with us as adults.

How Education Has Let Us Down

Who taught you how to speak in public? Probably your high school English teacher, though maybe you took a public speaking class in college or attended Toastmasters. In any event, like me, you were probably taught to use outdated strategies such as note cards, to write out the entire speech, to look over everyone's head, to walk around, and to put your presentation on a PowerPoint. These are just some of the many ineffective strategies still being taught in our public schools and universities today. Indeed, some of my adult clients say their K–12 speaking experiences actually left them unable to speak in front of other adults.

It's fair to note that not all school systems and teachers miss the mark. For example, a local charter school in my community teaches children as young as five to stand in front of their peers in an auditorium setting; this allows students to spend lots of time just getting comfortable being on stage. The school's director understands the value of building speaking into the curriculum every day in non-threatening ways. These students also learn how to express themselves in a safe environment by participating in group decision-making exercises in front of large groups of peers.

Activities such as Odyssey of the Mind, 4-H, Junior Achievement, children's theatre, and churches also encourage children to share their thoughts and stories in a safe environment.

These opportunities aside, the movement that began sometime in the 1980s called "writing and speaking across the university curriculum" greatly contributed to our collectively negative experiences with public speaking.

To fulfill the goal of writing and speaking across the curriculum, all college courses had to include writing and at least one speaking assignment. The problem was that professors outside the field of speech communication didn't know how to teach public speaking. Consequently, they relied on technology rather than real speaking techniques, instructing their students to place information in PowerPoint presentations to be read to the class.

Students' grades were normally not affected by how well they presented the material orally; they were graded on what was actually written in their PowerPoints. It became a given that students weren't good at speaking and, further, that teaching them how to speak fell well outside the realm and timeline for learning environmental science or world history or whatever course they happened to be taking. PowerPoint fulfilled the requirement. Amen.

Teaching public speaking is tricky. There is a critical balance between performance and self-concept, between learning effective techniques and using powerful material. Effective teachers know that classes must remain small so that each student has the maximum opportunity to speak.

However, there's a great deal more that hasn't been incorporated into the field, and this hurts all of us, teachers and students alike. For example, students are still expected to write full sentence outlines, which means they are still writing out virtually their entire presentations. At first blush this seems okay, but what happens is that the brain locks onto the words it creates and tries to remember exact sentences.

This is why people who write out their speeches tend to "sound" memorized and to get lost easier than those who do not write out their speeches. The more they write and re-write, the more their brains try to recall exact words. This is also why it's so hard for these individuals to speak conversationally.

As I am writing this now, I have the luxury of stopping to edit my sentences. I can use the thesaurus to find better words. I can play with structure. When writing, I am a wordsmith who crafts and shapes my thoughts.

When speaking, I don't have that luxury. I have to rely on a completely different set of skills to clearly communicate my ideas. Ironically, as a speaker, writing moves me in the wrong direction because it leads to memorization, and memorization leads to forgetting.

Real changes in methodology still need to emerge from within the field of speech communication. Unfortunately, professors tend not to focus on this but rather on how to teach public speaking in a mass learning environment. This is because, in most communication departments, public speaking is a cash cow. It is required of everyone who receives a college degree, so classes are designed to hold as many students as possible – thus the focus on mass learning. Most major universities hand these required, entry-level public speaking courses over to graduate students or to assistant professors new in the field.

The result is that while the methodology for teaching public speaking needs an overhaul, it isn't likely to get one.

Fear and the Professional: "I don't know Jack!"

If public speaking is public fear number one, what is number two? For professionals, it is the fear of being "found out." What if someone discovers we're not as "buttoned up" as we appear to be?

If we're honest, we'll admit that we all want the world to see us as competent, smart, confident, and decisive. Once we hit this level of performance, we want to protect this image, and with good reason.

The scenario goes something like this: you enjoy meeting with clients, you're great one on one, and you handle the boardroom with uncanny stealth. All is cool until you are invited to speak at the next conference. Then panic sets in, you lose sleep trying to figure out what to say,

you write too much, you begin to wonder if you can read from a teleprompter, and you pray for an illness so horrific that people will weep in the streets. Your cool exterior dissolves into a puddle on the floor.

Seth Godin in *The Big Moo* writes, "How to be a failure... Don't bother to dramatically increase the quality of your presentation style."

This statement stands out because it's true. It matters not where you are today in life. You may be a top executive delivering to a board of directors or a parent speaking to the board of education. Either way, your ability to capture the attention of others and speak clearly is a life survival skill.

Fear and Time In

There is yet another reason we experience high levels of anxiety when speaking in public, and it's simply because most of us have very little practice doing it. We all know that the more we engage in any type of activity, the more comfortable we become. Our central nervous systems actually calm down when we learn how to do something and practice it in a safe environment.

Take driving. Do you remember the first time you sat behind the wheel of a car? I'll bet your central nervous system was on high alert. However, over time, you stopped being so painfully aware. The same is true with many things we eventually become comfortable enough doing to take for granted.

Remember being sixteen and ordering a meal, leaving a voice message, or answering a question in public? I know; I have teenage grandchildren. It's painful to watch them muddle through these tasks, yet over time, they get better at them.

The same is true with speaking in public. It takes practice to get good at it. In later chapters, I'll present the skill sets you need to develop, but for now, please know upfront that you must put your time in for true change to occur.

Mind, Body, and Fear, or "The Network"

The central nervous system consists of a network of interconnected nerves that encompass the brain. When stress stimulates the central nervous system, our bodies receive electrochemical signals. As the brain detects a given situation as stressful, our bodies act accordingly, usually quickly, and at an unconscious level.

Below, I break fear into three interconnected parts just to clarify the relationship a bit more. As the illustration shows, fear is physical and physiological, and when these two come together, they leave an emotional imprint.

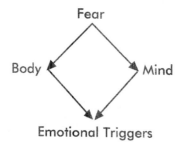

Fear Is Physical

When you are afraid, your heart rate increases, your blood pressure rises, and your eyes dilate. You shake, flush, and sweat in places you didn't know were possible. Your throat closes off, your breathing becomes shallow, and it's hard to think.

This experience is a result of your adrenal glands and your central nervous system going crazy; I call this an "adrenal dump."

What if I were to tell you that an adrenal dump is just that, an adrenal dump? It's not good or bad; it's neutral. Read on, and this will begin to make sense.

Fear Is Physiological

Simultaneously, as our bodies react to an event, our brains label it as good, bad, fun, horrible, exciting, excruciating, and so on. Let's use a rollercoaster as an example. Let's say we're at an amusement park, and I somehow talk you into riding the rollercoaster. As we strap in and start to hear the "Click, click, click" as our car climbs to the top, our central nervous systems begin soaring. Our hearts beat harder, and we both begin to sweat. I love it, so I'm smiling and screaming and laughing. You, however, are cursing, screaming, and crying.

When the ride ends, my first thought is, "Let's do it again!" Yours is, "I hate you!"

Both of us had an adrenal dump. Both of us experienced the typical physical sensations brought on by an adrenal dump. However, we labeled the experience differently, and this makes all the difference.

The psychology of fear is powerful stuff. It influences not only the here and now but it also impacts the future.

Fear and Our Emotional Triggers

When we combine the intensity of physical sensations with physiological labels, we are left with what I refer to as emotional imprints that lead to emotional triggers.

In other words, the brain holds memories that it reacts to even in new situations. Every time we find ourselves in a situation that simulates an earlier negative experience, our brains are unconsciously triggered on a physical as well as emotional level.

Once we start to have trigger reactions, one of two things happens. We either avoid all situations that trigger the same feelings (the flight response), or we learn new coping strategies and stay with the experience until we become desensitized to it (this is known as the fight response).

In his book *The New Earth, Awakening to Your Life's Purpose*, author Eckhart Tolle describes the mind as being "inherently dysfunctional." When I first read those words, I thought, "Well, Mr. Tolle, perhaps your mind is, but don't be calling dibs on mine."

Then I read on and began to understand his thinking. It goes something like this...

One of our greatest gifts is the gift of imagination. Our ability to imagine, insofar as we know, separates us from all other living creatures. Imagination is a limitless world, hindered only by the individuals engaged in it. However, did you know that your imagination, if left undisciplined, can actually work against you?

How many times have you found yourself daydreaming about an event that actually has not happened, yet you totally flip out?

Perhaps it's a conversation you need to have with your co-worker and you're afraid it won't go well so you play it out with negative results.

Maybe you're wired like me, so all of a sudden you imagine someone in your life dying. Before you know it, you're bawling your eyes out over something that hasn't happened.

Perhaps you had an argument with a friend, and weeks, months, or years later, you're still rehashing the scene and getting mad all over again.

Every one of these examples happens because our imaginations conjure up thoughts, conversations, images, and emotions that we react to as though they were real.

Where would we be today without great minds? Think of all the discoveries and breakthroughs in medicine and science that only come about because we have the ability to imagine. However, most of us tend to squander our minds by letting our thoughts wander wherever and whenever they please.

I often hear people comment on their short attention spans. We blame society, television, video games, and age, but what if, in most cases, our distraction is the result of not taking intentional control of where our thoughts go? This age-old concept of mind strengthening is as real and applicable today as it was two thousand years ago.

Ask yourself what your triggers are. How often do you allow your mind to drift into unproductive places? More importantly, what are you doing to reprogram your trigger cycle?

There's a great parable about a young ninja warrior who was told that she was to go into battle with Fear. As these words were spoken, Fear entered the room and swallowed the girl whole.

She could smell Fear and feel Fear on the nape of her neck. All sounds were drowned out by the roaring in her ears and the beating of her heart. She felt cold and sweaty. She tried to think, but she couldn't, so she did the only thing she could think of, and that was to bow.

In the martial arts, bowing is a sign of respect. When Fear saw the young girl bow, he was taken aback. No one had ever bowed to him before. He had entered that room hundreds of times, and always the young ninja had tried to fight. This girl was different.

Fear smiled at this brave soul and said, "Young warrior, since you were gracious enough to show me respect, I want to tell you the secret for battling me."

The girl took a step back, released a loud sigh, and carefully sat down to listen.

"You see," Fear explained, "my weapons are not those of swords; my weapons are far more lethal. When I enter, I'm all around you. I get right into your head, and then I begin my best work. I become your inner voice. I'm so good that you can't tell the difference between my voice and yours. Sometimes my voice sounds like your father, your mother, or that not-so-best friend from your childhood."

Fear continued, "My favorite voice is slightly above a whisper, as in 'Who do you think you are' and 'You can't pull that off' and 'People are going to see right through you.' Some of my other

12

favorites are, 'You just don't have what others have' and 'If you think you feel foolish, you should see how you look!'"

Fear stopped to allow the young ninja a chance to consider what he had told her.

The young warrior looked hard at Fear and began to smile just a little. "So it's you!" she said to Fear. "You're that voice I hear! I seem to hear it all the time."

"That's true," said Fear, "I do enjoy making a big entrance like I did when I came in here today, but my best work is more subtle."

The young ninja thought about this for a moment and then said, "You're actually a part of me, but if you're a part of me, what can I do to change this voice and your power?"

"Excellent question!" replied Fear. "You wish to hear the secret for battling me, but be warned – you won't be able to master it overnight. In fact, it takes a lifetime to achieve. The secret is, stop listening."

I can only imagine what you're thinking right now. "Just say stop" sounds very similar to the "Just say no" campaign against drugs, and we all know how well that worked. But stick with me here. The difference is the brain.

Current brain research reveals that our brains are continuously changing. Scientists used to believe our brains were hard programmed and that little changed after age five. It has only been in the last decade that neuroscientists have been able to go inside the brain and observe how learning actually occurs at the molecular level.

The brain is capable of learning and re-learning throughout the life span. When our brains are learning, synapses fire from different areas of the brain, and all our senses, including our emotions, become involved. Learning actually causes changes to the physical structure of the brain.

This is powerful information. It means we can change our brain patterns by changing what we focus on. Many of my clients feel that they can't control how they feel about public speaking. As soon as the word is mentioned, they have immediate negative thoughts. Brain research argues that we can change patterns.

How to "Stop Listening"

Let's go back to what Fear had to say to the young warrior: "Stop listening." It's so simple yet so very hard to accomplish. How many ways do you allow fear to be front and center in your life? How loud is your critical voice?

Awareness comes first. Personally, I have been working on "stop listening" for years. It's hard work. First, I've realized that I can't change anything I'm not first aware of, so I have to become aware that I'm allowing my mind to drift into areas that trigger negative emotions. Thus, the first step is awareness.

Consider your triggers about public speaking. When you are asked to give a report, what goes through your head? Perhaps you entertain thoughts such as the following: "I hate giving presentations. I'm always so nervous. I wonder if someone could fill in for me."

When these or similar thoughts begin, pay attention to how your body responds. Does your heart rate increase? If so, say "Stop." Say it out loud. Say it again and again and again.

You're actually beginning the process. It doesn't matter if you have to say "stop" hundreds of times a day; it all adds up. In the nanosecond that you tell yourself to stop, you are beginning to create new brain patterns.

Think of this as mind strengthening. Think of it as increasing your concentration and discipline. Think of it as possible and important and even life-changing work.

Say "Stop," but then what? Remember Stewart Smalley's daily affirmations with Al Franken on Saturday Night Live back in the 1990s? He would sit in front of a mirror, gaze at himself, and say, "I'm good enough, I'm smart enough, and, doggone it, people like me."

I know what you're thinking: "He's not very funny today; he should have stuck to Stewart Smalley!"

Perhaps this is true, but based on the latest brain research, Stewart was right after all. It does matter what you say to yourself.

Say "I'm excited!" instead of "I'm nervous!" "I'm nervous." Say those words over and over. What begins to happen to your body? Most likely, you begin to feel nervous.

Words are powerful, so choose your words wisely. I ask my clients to replace "I'm nervous" with "I'm excited." I suggest this because it works. Your body doesn't know the difference between negative and positive stress; what matters is how you label it. Just try it. See what happens when you say "I'm excited" instead of "I'm nervous."

I once had a client show up for class wearing a t-shirt that read "I'm excited" on the day he gave his first presentation. He said he couldn't help but laugh every time he looked down at it.

To say you're excited when you're actually nervous messes with your memory board and temporarily stops programmed triggers from firing.

My husband, whom I love to the moon and back, has a habit of saying, "Aren't you nervous about your upcoming presentation?" I say, "No, I'm excited." He says, "I'd be nervous." I say, "That's okay, but I'm excited." He says, "Wow, I'd really be nervous." I say, "lock it down, I got this."

See, "stop" can be verbalized in more ways than one!

Stop focusing on what's not working. Ah, feedback...Not just any old feedback, but negative feedback. Everyone wants it. They beg for it. They want to know exactly what they're doing wrong. If you're a member of Toastmasters, you know people actually do count "ums" and track mistakes.

I'm an anomaly. I do not give my clients negative feedback. Decades of experience have taught me that it doesn't create positive results. If you are ready to click off and request your money back, please hear me out. I've been teaching public speaking since 1982, and I feel strongly that negative feedback only creates more of what's not working. One reason I left the traditional classroom is that I didn't find it useful to attach grades to presentations, and I'm not alone. A growing body of research argues that negative feedback actually leads to a greater increase in the undesirable behavior.

I do believe in feedback; I just utilize it differently. Feedback is powerful when it's used to fine-tune or adjust speaking skills. A good teacher in any subject understands that first you teach and then you reinforce the skill. In Chapter Nine, for example, I lay out a very specific set of skills all public speakers need to use.

Do yourself a huge favor and learn these skills. Practice how to stand, how to hold notes, how to preview, and how to review. Learn how to use stories and make real eye contact. Focus on skills you're doing well and ask yourself why this skill is working for you. Have people you trust watch you and ask them where your skills are the strongest.

The need for negative feedback is so strong that I've have clients ask to meet with me after class to give them negative feedback. I tell them the worst thing they can do is seek such feedback. The skills used in public speaking are actually really simple; the hard part is to let go of the crazy need to focus on the negative and to replace this need with skill-based practice.

Chapter Summary

All speakers experience adrenaline dumps and moments of "What just happened?" However, skills, concentration, and practice can keep those moments just that…moments. If you believe you're the only one experiencing issues with public speaking, your belief simply isn't grounded in reality.

Yes, fear is real, and it affects everyone physically, emotionally, and psychologically. It will follow you into the boardroom and onto the stage. There are no short cuts to changing fear patterns, but there is work you can do to begin the process of recalibrating your triggers. You can make it happen, and the ball is in your court.

Chapter Two:

The Myth of Perfection

Perfection doesn't receive a lot of party invites. She's perplexed by this.
—Onlee Bowden

A myth is a set of beliefs that frame our thoughts and actions. Many myths go unchallenged, making us co-conspirators as we reinforce them through our own unconscious behaviors.

A crippling myth fogs our relationship with public speaking and leaves us feeling out of control and anxious. This is the myth of perfection, and this chapter explores how to begin the work of replacing it with something more authentic.

The Myth of Perfect versus Organized and Real

Research in the field of communication sheds light on what happens when we stand up to speak. As we stand, we separate ourselves from our peers. The very act of standing suggests that we, the speaker, are above the group. As a general rule, we are far more comfortable and at ease when sitting. This is why most people prefer meeting settings to other public speaking formats.

19

This phenomenon of separating ourselves from our peers leads to the deep-seated belief that in order to earn the right to stand, we must be perfect. When we imagine ourselves as perfect speakers, we envision flawless presentations with no "ums," no loss of words, and no hesitations. We over-write and over-rehearse to get it just right, and when we finish, we weigh the worth of our speeches on how many mistakes we did or did not commit.

The reality is that because humans are inherently flawed, there is nothing about communication that is perfect, yet we continue to strive for perfection in an inherently imperfect medium. Why do we reach for the impossible? I suggest it's because we buy into the myth that we must be perfect to be valued as speakers.

Don't misunderstand my point; I want perfection if I'm having surgery, getting my car fixed, or having work done on my house. Perfection has its proper place, but it's simply not achievable when communicating.

When I was younger, things that were messy and muddled bothered me because I wanted perfection. Truly, I love perfection, and I come to this very organically. My father suffered from obsessive compulsive disorder, and through him, I embraced my own focus on perfection. I really wanted to be perfect in all that I did. This need left me deeply critical of myself as well as too easily hurt by others.

I didn't appreciate how ingrained this preference was until I was diagnosed with a brain tumor. Not only was I bombarded with migraines, but I couldn't find my words. Me! A speaker, teacher, and corporate professional unable to remember what I wanted to say!

In the beginning, I stressed about this and felt self-conscious to the point of shutting down. My anxiety grew exponentially until finally I sought help. This is when everything changed for me, and for the better. Now I feel graced with humility, and after all these years of teaching, I finally get it. Real is more important than perfect.

To further my lesson, sometime after I recovered from my brain tumor, I was diagnosed with MCI, mild cognitive impairment. Short of a brain injury, it's most prevalent in families stricken with Alzheimer's, which is the case in my family.

MCI is almost always progressive, and it leaves me with days that I struggle. Many times, I'll be in front of a group when the next word or phrase that I want flies out of my head.

Because I rely on a very easy-to-follow organizational structure that allows me to use at-a-glance speaking notes to clean up my thoughts and get me moving forward, I am able to recover and go on.

I finally understand where perfection fits and where it doesn't. I know that being organized and compelling is what resonates with my audience. I trust myself to be real. This allows me to relax, and just the act of relaxing helps my synapses to fire.

What Happens When We Believe in the Myth?

When we strive for perfection as speakers, we make decisions that lead to failure. For example, as I mentioned earlier, in the pursuit of perfection, people write out their presentations. The myth is that writing leads to clearer thoughts and thus more confidence, so people write and re-write and wordsmith until they have it just right…In fact, until they have it perfect!

Alas, when it's time to speak, these same individuals are hyper-focused on remembering their exact phrases because these phrases were, after all, perfect. The problem is, unless they have photographic memories, they are likely to forget what they wrote. In fact, extreme blanking out often occurs because writing is for reading, not for speaking. It doesn't lead to a perfect speech, yet the desire for perfection still sends people down this path.

A funny twist on perfection occurs when speakers are afraid someone in the audience knows more about their topic than they do. It's more than likely that certain people in any given audience do know more than the speaker. To combat this, speakers sometimes throw everything they have at their audience in an attempt to sound smart and be perfect. The result is an audience that feels bombarded and confused.

Organized, clear, and real trumps perfection every time. Public speaking pulls from our most used and most effective core communication skills, such as making others feel comfortable, thinking on our feet, letting go of distracting thoughts, organizing our thoughts, and paying genuine attention to others. These are core skills for all communication, and we need to utilize them every single day, whether we are building relationships or giving a speech.

The word core means "the middle," "the center," "the source of all strength and growth." Core communication skills are within your reach, and when you're stronger at your core, you're just plain stronger overall. I've had clients who were uncomfortable answering the phone or handling a customer issue who, after taking public speaking training, experienced a dramatic shift in their abilities across the spectrum.

Chapter Summary

Being real is more impressive than being perfect. Don't buy into the myth. Learn the skill sets for speaking and spend time practicing them so you can trust your body and your mind when you're speaking.

Chapter Three:

Communication Truths and Speaking in Public

Truth walks with a little bounce in her step and her shoulders relaxed because she feels a deep sense of freedom.

-Onlee Bowden

We often feel we are victims of public speaking. We often see ourselves as static or trapped in styles that do not serve us well when we stand in front of others. Sometimes we even look at other speakers and resent their ease or ability to pull others into their presentations. These moments seem to magnify our feelings of inadequacy and increase our belief that we just weren't made to give speeches.

However, what if I were to tell you that you actually have a tremendous amount of control as a speaker? The fact is, public speaking is rooted in communication, and communication is rooted in universal truths. Because we are born into communication, we tend not to view it as anything more than an extension of our personalities. Although our personalities are unique and do impact our communication styles, communication is its own discipline.

Thanks to those who have committed their professional lives to the study of communication, we know for a fact that communication is learned, flawed, dynamic, messy, essential, and impossible to avoid. This chapter will explore some of these truths about communication and explain how to begin using them to enhance your presentation style.

The Truth: Communication Is Learned

You, me, the person sitting next to you, and everyone else was "born" into communication. Once born, our family cultures mixed with our personality traits and molded us as communicators. The result: some people are extraverts, some are introverts, some are demonstrative, and others keep to themselves. Some people are loud, and some are quiet.

Why are our communication styles so different? Mostly because of how we were taught:

- "I was raised to believe you never talked about money."

- "I was raised to always say 'please' and 'thank you.'"

- "I was raised not to pay much attention to manners."

- "I was raised to fight for what I want."

- "I was raised to always make eye contact."

- "I was raised to never make eye contact."

- "I was raised to never cry in public."

- "I was raised to voice my opinion no matter what."

- "I was raised to get everything off my chest."

- "I was raised to believe I didn't have anything worth saying."

- "I was raised to never talk about family issues."

We were all raised somewhere, by people who powerfully influenced how we communicate. You see, besides a handful of universal nonverbal behaviors such as smiling and crying, we have all learned how to communicate.

If communication is learned, it can also be re-learned, and this is the good news. Communication patterns can be changed. Who you are as a communicator, as a speaker, can be re-learned.

This good news is also the difficult news because it puts the onus for change on you. No one holds the patent on communication, and you don't need permission to expand your skill set. It's simply something you have to want to do.

Ask those who were shy how they changed. They will say that, at some point, they just started to act more self-assured. They had to step out of their comfort zones and take a chance. They will also tell you that it didn't feel very good at first, but the longer they did it, the easier it became.

You have to want the change more than you want the current situation to continue. If you see someone speaking who makes great eye contact and you know this is an issue for you, study this individual. Then, the next time you're in front of a group, force yourself to copy this person and make more eye contact. It really is that simple.

Ask yourself two questions:

One: are you ready to give yourself permission to shed some communication patterns that work against you as a speaker?

Two: are you ready to give yourself permission to try some new ways of communicating?

As a speech trainer, I hear people say, "It's not my style to have bigger gestures or to speak with more volume." Or I hear, "I'm just naturally soft-spoken; I can't speak louder."

How do you feel about such comments now that you know communication is learned?

The Truth: You Can't Not Communicate

Even when we don't think we're sending a message, our nonverbal behavior is saying something. Every aspect of our being including our hair, scent, dress, mannerisms, jewelry, posture, eye contact, facial expressions, vocal tones, how we walk, and even how we stand sends messages loaded with meaning. Bottom line: we are always communicating.

My goal in Flip It on Its Ear is to help you develop a set of presentation skills that are consistent with the message you intend to send. For example, if you want your audience to receive the message that you are confident and at ease, you need to develop a set of nonverbal and verbal skills that authentically reinforce the message "I am confident and at ease."

The Truth: Communication Is Dynamic

We can never repeat the same situation in exactly the same way because time, people, and situations change from moment to moment.

Think about a time you told a good story and the people listening were completely engaged. A while later, when you told what you believed was exactly the same story, with all the same bells and whistles, you received a completely different response. This is usually when you say, "Well, I guess you had to be there."

What really happened is that, like a continuously flowing river, you were not in the same place twice, so what worked one moment didn't work the next.

This truth about communication gives us useful insight into the importance of being a good listener when we are speaking. We have to listen carefully to our audience so we can adjust our message to better fit the changing situation.

Chapter Summary

Communication is learned. You can't not communicate, and communication is dynamic. Therefore, people who rely heavily on their notes or on doing something exactly as they practiced it run a very large risk of missing the mark as a speaker. Instead, the key is to dial into others and adjust, adjust, adjust.

Chapter Four:

Public Speaking and the Bottom Line

She finally convinced Bottom Line that Relationship was his best friend.

-Onlee Bowden

Successful businesses grow by building relationships, and people choose to do business with those whom they know, like, and trust. How do folks get to know you and your services and begin relying on you as a valuable resource?

The answer boils down to this: you have to be visible. You have to be where your customers are. More than that, you have to be in front of them in a variety of ways: presenting at school board meetings, volunteering in your community, explaining your services, being active in your local chamber, co-presenting with other professionals, and accepting any and all opportunities to get on the radio or participate in panel discussions.

Yet how many times have you declined such opportunities? How many times have your employees declined them? How comfortable is your staff with promoting your business?

Here are a few examples of what can happen when you start to say "yes" to public speaking opportunities.

A great friend and client of mine is Terry Umlor, the owner of Springfield Roofing. Several years back, I met Terry when his company was nominated for a Small Business of the Year award. Shortly thereafter, I received a phone call from Terry's wife, who had taken my course, asking if I would work with Terry to help him prepare for a "Meet the Candidate" breakfast.

Terry ran a successful company and had gained a reputation as a humanitarian in our community, but he wasn't at all prepared for what was about to happen to him. Indeed, he readily admitted that he preferred to stay behind the scenes and avoid any situation involving speaking. Now he had to be front and center, promoting his values, philosophy, and company.

Not only did Terry win the Small Business of the Year award, but this was only the beginning. He went on to be named to the list of the fifty most watched companies in the state of Michigan! More recently, he served on the board of directors for the Traverse City Chamber of Commerce. These are just the highlights; there is much, much more, and it all came about because he finally said "yes" to speaking in public.

The Bank of Northern Michigan and its sister bank, The Bank of Holland, made a commitment to public speaking training more than four years ago. All their employees received level one training, and key people received level two. Why? Because management believed all people who work for the bank should be able to answer the question, "Why should I bank with you?"

Now these organizations are taking it to the next level. They are training people to be able to go into service organizations to talk about business-related topics and using gorilla marketing to position themselves in front of their target markets. This is a huge commitment to public speaking training, and organizations are seeing the payoffs.

Hagerty Insurance is a niche company with an international presence that specializes in insuring collector automobiles and vintage boats. This forward-thinking organization has developed more than just a training arm to its business; it has created an actual university that offers career-oriented employees many avenues for professional advancement. Since 2007, public speaking has been a part of Hagerty U, and employees from all areas of the business take the course. Again, why would a company of this magnitude invest so heavily and openly in public speaking? It sees the payoff.

Another example is Oneup Web, an award-winning digital marketing agency with over twenty years of experience and expertise. This firm has allocated precious resources to train everyone in the agency in public speaking as well as to offer specialized training in how to present on screen and in interactive meetings with clients. The reason: everyone has face time with clients in one way or another, and Oneup believes in a seamless brand of "Be Relentless." The company needs people who are strong enough to question the status quo with clients and with each other. It simply can't afford to have employees who are afraid to speak up.

Now let's look at the other side of the coin and examine what happens when an organization doesn't understand the relationship between public speaking and the bottom line.

Several years back, I worked with a company that participated in trade shows. It spent big bucks on a fancy booth with various bells and whistles but manned it, essentially, with robots. I don't mean literal robots; I mean people who were too socially inept to pull potential customers in. These guys could stand there and smile, but they couldn't engage in small talk. They couldn't reach out, make customers comfortable, and pull them in.

My question was, why bother going to trade shows? Why spend hard-earned money on marketing when you can't finish the job? The company noticed no return on investing in trade shows and dropped them from their strategic plan.

Another local firm in my hometown allows its employees to answer the phone with "Hello" and nothing more. Pure silence follows this perfunctory greeting. Callers don't even know if they have the right business, let alone with whom they're speaking.

The result? This company hasn't grown in over twenty years and is still plunking along, apparently content to be "good enough."

The person who answers the call is either rude, lacks basic training, or is extremely shy, but in the end, it doesn't really matter. The outcome is the same. (As an aside, it's interesting to note that shy people are almost always perceived as rude even when that's not their intention.)

When our mortgage was sold to a nationally known lender, my first call from them was so rude and remedial that I threw some big words down and hung up. Later, while talking with a friend, she said she'd had the same experience. It made me wonder if all this company's clients are forced into the relationship through buy-outs. My guess is yes, because the company certainly isn't earning customers based on its communication skills.

Here's my last example, although I could go on and on. A local sandwich shop serves fantastic subs, but they come at a price – dealing with the impatient people who take your order. They kind of scare me, and I have to feel ready when I go in to order. It's like having our very own "Soup Nazi" shades of Seinfeld right here at home, but instead of "No soup for you!" it's "No sub for you!"

Thanks to all these examples, you can probably guess my vitally important takeaway question: how is the person who answers your phone or takes your money doing at building relationships for your business?

It's interesting to note that most businesses spend the majority of their training budgets on managers and leaders and not on the people who have the most contact with customers. At first blush, this may not appear to be related to public speaking, but it actually has everything to do with public speaking.

Any time a person is interacting with the public, it is public speaking. This includes everything from answering the phone to taking an order to taking money to giving a speech. Each type of public speaking can cause fear, and each person's level of comfort is individual, so to narrowly define the role of public speaking in your organization is to take a really big risk of losing your market share.

Chapter Summary

I've been providing various types of training to organizations since the 1980s in the areas of customer service, conflict management, and teamwork. Most of it isn't worth the money spent on it.

Today, I only train in public speaking because it's hands-on, focuses on real skills, and makes a critical difference to the bottom line. Nonetheless, real change in communication cannot and does not happen merely by thinking about it; it has to be put on and worn like a pair of new shoes. Sure, they feel uncomfortable at first, but over time they have the potential to feel like an old friend.

Ready to begin the process of preparing yourself for public speaking? Turn the page and let's begin.

Part Two:

You on Skills, or How to Become an Effective Speaker

He remembered when Brave was just a little boy;
he was always first in line and eager.
-Onlee Bowden

art Two puts you back in the game with the specific skills and strategies you need to design and prepare a presentation. It begins with a closer look at how your audience forms your message and then examines the role concentration plays in speaking effectively.

Next, this section presents a set of skills designed to give you more control over your body when you're in front of others, with each skill broken down into easy-to-incorporate, everyday behaviors such as standing or gestures.

Finally, this section lays out a client-proven, at-a-glance method for organizing a presentation.

The philosophy behind Part Two is that speakers are made, not born. Everyone has the right to learn what is involved in creating a message, and this section is dedicated to providing that understanding by removing the veil surrounding public speaking and giving you client-proven techniques you can use immediately.

Chapter Five:

It's all about the Audience

Audience is often bored with herself. She tries to be more interested, but that just makes her want to take a nap.

- Onlee Bowden

Ever heard the old expression, "If Momma ain't happy, ain't nobody happy"? Think of your audience as your momma. Even a brilliant idea can be derailed by an unresponsive audience.

To reduce misfires with your message, take time to consider whom you're speaking to. In textbooks, you will find concepts like "audience analysis." This can be an effective tool for knowing who you're speaking to, but with respect to your already full schedule, it's not helpful to have to undergo a lengthy process in order to gain insight.

With this in mind, I've narrowed your audience analysis down to just a few questions you should answer before you start to plan a presentation.

Perhaps the most important question is this: why is this individual or group interested in what you're saying? Not why are you interested in the topic, mind you, but why are they interested? What's in it for them?

Base your answer on who they are and how they are connected to your topic. Once you understand this, you can choose stories, examples, and main points that convey your message in terms they can relate to. Knowing your audience helps you choose the best way to design your message.

For example, you can't take a message about local economic growth that worked for the chamber of commerce's young professional group and assume it will have the same impact in front of a group of church elders. Both groups want to know the information but for different reasons; your job is to determine what those reasons are and to deliver a message crafted to them.

Because no two audiences are the same, we never deliver the same message twice.

Understanding this can save you some serious heartache. I remember years ago presenting to a trucking company in Detroit. This group was thinking about joining a truckers' union, and the owners wanted to try one more approach before this happened. My job was to present a system called gain-sharing. This was critical information, and the truckers had the option of either trying or refusing this approach. We worked for weeks on the best way to present the information and then we made the drive into downtown Detroit and entered a company totally surrounded by razor wire. Two women in their thirties were entering the belly of the beast.

Our first presentation went so stinkin' smoothly that I was certain we had this thing nailed. There was a lot of interest and buy-in, and I decided this wasn't going to be so hard after all. My colleague and I went to lunch after the presentation and came back fat, dumb, and happy. That's how we referred to it after that, because the second group we presented to bore no resemblance to the first.

Directly in the front row sat this really big guy with his arms crossed. As I was laying out the program, he kept leaning over to the guys next to him and laughing. I finally asked him what was up, and he said, "Lady, do you really want me to tell you what's up? I think all of this is a bunch of bull###!!!***."

Silence…Man, was I fat, dumb, and happy!

How did I handle that moment? I knew what I did next was critical. Anger or defensiveness would do nothing in my favor, and this man was probably just saying out loud what many others were thinking.

I stayed calm and showed him respect. I thanked him for his candor and acknowledged his feelings. I told him there were probably others feeling exactly as he did.

He appreciated my approach and relaxed some with me, and then I asked him for a favor. Would he be willing to hear the idea through, and if at the end he felt it was worth considering, would he take a leadership role in making gain-sharing happen in his company?

He agreed to listen and he liked the concept. Sure enough, he helped lead the rollout for his company. It's been over twenty years now, and I have no idea what has become of the company, but the experience has remained with me. Today, as then, I strive to show respect to all audience members and to remember that every single audience is unique, which means I need to meet them where they are.

Audience Members Are Listeners, and Listeners Are Bad at Their Jobs!

Human beings have the incredible ability to process around seven hundred words per minute, yet we talk at about three hundred words per minute. This ability, which I discuss in more detail in the next chapter, is called thought-speed. Thought-speed makes us distracted listeners. Rather than use thought-speed time more productively by controlling our desire to drift and daydream, we typically spend that time thinking about what we're going to say next or what we're planning for dinner or what our friends are doing. Thus, my mantra is, "Audience members are listeners, and listeners are bad at their jobs." Let me clarify that audience members are not bad people; they're just bad at the job of listening.

Listening is actually a fluid skill that changes depending on the occasion. For example, if you're with a best friend and she says she needs to talk about a problem, you are likely to use your best listening skills to block out distractions and concentrate on what she is saying. But if you're sitting about a third of the way back from the podium listening to the company president give an update or motivational talk or explain new strategies for the next quarter, listening is an entirely different animal.

It's easy to drift and daydream in a crowd. We don't feel personally responsible for giving encouraging feedback to the speaker because we have people to the right and left who can do that. Thus, at any given point in a presentation, various audience members aren't listening.

What can I say? It's a really hard pill to swallow, but it's better to accept it than pretend it's not happening.

For this reason, as I've mentioned multiple times, your number one goal as a speaker is to get and keep your audience's attention.

Don't Let Any Single Listener Rock Your Boat

Most audience members are not aware of the messages they are sending. Here's a true story that illustrates that you don't know what you don't know. This was my wake-up moment as a speaker.

Years ago, I was the keynote speaker at a conference. The room offered stadium seating, so I was at the bottom, looking up at my audience. I was giving a motivational speech designed to get people recharged. About three-quarters of the way up and to my left sat a dark-haired woman who caught my attention because she looked truly angry. At first I ignored her, and then I found myself checking her out when the audience was laughing to see if her expression changed. Nothing. In fact, she often frowned while others smiled. Before my presentation ended, I decided I hated her. Actually I was rattled by her and dumbfounded by her response. It seemed over the top for the type of presentation I was delivering. This was a motivational keynote speech, nothing heavy, nothing earthshattering.

When the presentation ended, people hung around to talk. To my surprise, I saw her waiting in line. As you can imagine, I wasn't terribly keen on talking with her. I figured she disagreed with something I'd said, and I didn't want to have that discussion in front of others.

Finally, I had no choice. She was next in line, so I prepared myself for the worst. Here is what she said: "Hi, Onlee. I really feel we have so much in common, and I wanted to thank you for speaking."

So much for my astute powers of observation. So much for not allowing a single individual to rock my boat. So much for not taking it personally.

So what happened? Well, sometimes paying attention and not paying attention look very similar. Sometimes when we are concentrating on a speaker, our faces look angry because we frown to concentrate. Other times, stories shared by the speaker trigger memories of our own lives, and we show these feelings on our faces. At still other times, we wear neutral expressions because we're daydreaming and not tuned it.

The issue is that neutral faces generally look bored and/or angry. Rarely are they friendly looking. That's why it's tough not to get caught in the trap. As speakers, we just don't know what's going on behind the faces of the individuals in our audience. To read these faces as negative isn't necessarily accurate.

Generally, audience members aren't trying to give positive or negative feedback. They are simply listening, so when you look out at a sea of neutral faces, don't take what you see personally.

Do Your Part to Pull Your Audience In

Even though a case can be made that poor audience behavior is, in part, no fault of your own, you do have a responsibility to do your best to understand why your audience may be inattentive.

Below are several key considerations for getting and keeping your audience.

• **Stay Alert:** Never assume you can give the same presentation twice and get the same exact response. All audiences bring their own vibe and need to be met where they are. Stay alert and pay attention to the ebb and flow of your here-and-now presentation. Keep your mind calm yet energized and ready to adapt.

• **Stay Tuned In:** Tune into outside distractions. If the room starts to feel a little sluggish, it's harder for others to pay attention. Figure out what's happening and try to address it if possible. How is the room arranged? Can you see everyone, or do some people have their backs to you? How warm is the room? It's best to have the room slightly on the cool side when meetings begin; people will warm it up as time passes. Consider the time of day the presentation is being held. Mornings are best. After lunch or later in the day is when most people experience lower levels of energy. What can you do to compensate for this?

- **Stay Energized:** To keep the audience's energy up, raise your energy level. Breathe deeper, find your stance, and smile broader. Speak with a twinkle in your voice and eyes. People will respond, and the room will feel lighter.

- **Stay Interesting:** Make sure you have something worthwhile to say, and keep your message fresh and current. Focus on being visually interesting and engaging by utilizing the speaking triangle I introduce later in Chapter Nine.

- **Stay Together:** Get organized, stay organized, and speak your organization using the structure and skills presented later in this section.

- **Stay Connected:** Connect to your audience. Think about what people need and want and give it to them. Always use compelling stories and examples they can relate to.

- **Stay Ahead:** If the topic is controversial, don't be afraid to talk about the elephant in the room, and be prepared to field questions with respect and clarity.

- **Stay Inviting:** Demonstrate how you want to interact with your audience by modeling. Smile, use a calm but energized voice, make real eye contact, and send the message, "Come on in, the water's fine." Laugh at yourself and see your own humor. Show that you're safe and that people can trust you. Remember, people believe non-verbal messages over the spoken word.

Everyone Has Someone

It's hard to imagine, but everyone has someone who makes them nervous, and we all sweat just a little more when that person is in the audience. Top executives have board members. Others react to friends, co-workers, or family members in the audience. Still others are thrown off their game by the size of the audience. Perhaps the stakes are high and you feel a lot is riding on this moment. Everyone has that moment and/or that person.

When that person is in your audience, fear begins to speak loudly. Without meaning to, you may feel a need to impress, get the moment just right, or not let someone down. These thoughts can result in you feeling more vulnerable than you normally do. Fears about public speaking and the need to be perfect creep in. You will have a strong desire to bail on everything you learn in this course. I want to encourage you to keep the faith and get your skill sets firmly in place so you can rise to the occasion.

When we speak, we bring a lot of mental junk to the podium. Who is in your audience and why you're speaking is certainly part of that junk. We all have pressure points, and like so many aspects to becoming a more effective sharer of ideas, we benefit greatly when we build an internal monitoring system to calm and energize us.

Chapter Summary

Remember, audience members are listeners, and listeners are bad at their jobs. Realistically, most audience members aren't aware that they're making you nervous. Try to remember that crowd behavior isn't always conducive to putting you at ease and that most people aren't conscious of the non-verbal messages they are sending.

Often, when we're part of an audience, we engage in lazy listener habits. We drift and daydream and allow our minds to run willy-nilly. Because of this, audiences often demonstrate awful listening skills, and this can be a hard hurdle to overcome.

Take hold of what you can do to reduce disconnect with your audience. Make your presentation more meaningful. Understand what makes your audience tick. Discover valuable insights to guide your main points and stories by remembering to ask a few valuable questions about your audience.

Also begin to accept that some audiences have more emotional and professional pull on your psyche than others. When faced with more risky speaking occasions, be ready.

Finally, remember that you can dramatically increase your effectiveness with your audience when you think of yourself as a host and less like a talking head. Invite your audience into your presentation by throwing out a calm, energized, and trustful demeanor. Take care of your audience by putting them first. Greet people before a presentation with a warm handshake and some small talk. Meet people at the conference room door and welcome them. Above all, let your underlying message be, "Come on in, the water's fine."

Chapter Six:

The Art of Concentration

Concentration is bewildered. He used to be so popular and everyone expected him to show up. What happened?
- Onlee Bowden

Do you ever feel that concentration is an elusive character that flitters about without any concern for the task at hand? I hope you're nodding, because a break in concentration is the number one reason we get lost when speaking in front of others.

It's frustrating to feel so out of sorts with something as basic as concentration, but it isn't hard to see how it happens. As a nation, we are having a torrid affair with concentration's twin brother, distraction. We seek this twin and welcome it at every turn. We blame distractions when it's convenient, of course, but welcome them with open arms when we are overwhelmed.

As a society, our concentration levels continue to drop as our susceptibility to distraction deepens. Blame it on electronics, television, or any other concentration-sucking aspect of our culture.

The fact is, it's a real issue, especially when we're speaking in front of others.

When I speak to groups on the topic of public speaking, I talk about what it means to stay "inside" a presentation. This is a way of imagining where your head should be when you're speaking. Simply put, your thoughts need to be completely focused on the here and now.

Two years ago, my oldest grandson was in his senior year of high school and playing varsity basketball. His undefeated small-town team won districts and moved on to the regional finals. All season, I was full of nerves watching the team play, yet no matter how much the heat was turned up, the team played strong. It was in the zone, fully focused, and concentrating on the job at hand.

Most of us have experienced this feeling in one form or the other. Maybe for you it occurs when you play music or golf. Perhaps yoga, dance, fishing, or some other sport is your "in the zone" activity. However you've experienced it, it's what you're reaching for when you're speaking in front of others. As a speaker, when you're "in the zone," you stay inside your presentation, which means you stay focused on the moment and don't jump ahead or re-hash what you just said. Staying inside your presentation means blocking out what doesn't matter and zeroing in on what does. Organization, clarity, stories, and pace; this is where your head needs to be.

Whether we are aware of it or not, those who understand the art of concentration are the speakers we most enjoy listening to. They seem at ease with themselves and are able to find their words quickly. They have a way of making us feel comfortable, and they know when to move the presentation along or when to insert just the right story. These presenters have fine-tuned the discipline of concentration.

Concentration is the ability to focus on whatever it is you choose for the length of time you choose it. Concentration is the mind's ability to filter information quickly and to act on it. In the East, it's called mind strengthening.

When you concentrate, you stay focused on the present, on the here and now. In other words, you don't allow your mind to race ahead or to entertain you with sideline commentary. Distractions are simply nonexistent when a speaker is in the zone.

Imagine yourself in the zone. You're not worried, not hyper focused on what is happening to your body, not listening to your critical voice. Rather, you pay close attention to the exchange between you and your audience. You listen to your own stories and examples and enjoy them as if you're telling them for the first time. Your focus is on the moment and the people in front of you.

Remember the concept called thought-speed I mentioned in the last chapter? It means that your brain processes information about three times faster than you speak. In essence, thought-speed is how you mentally finish someone's sentence and drift off into subjects of greater personal interest way before the speaker actually finishes his or her idea.

When you speak in public, the same problem occurs. Your brain can finish your thoughts much faster than you speak, allowing you to race ahead or begin engaging in self-talk. The problem is that your brain really can't be in two places at once, at least not with respect to communication. As soon as you leave the present conversation, you have broken your concentration.

The crazy thing about concentration is that only you can improve it, so here's your challenge. Go into a coffee shop and sit down to read a book for ten minutes. Your goal is to concentrate, so let go of any noise that comes into your ears. Pay no attention to what's going on around you. Choose not to acknowledge the stimulus. Just read. Focus. Take notes or highlight what you're reading. Think about what you're reading.

Or, alternatively, go sit in a crowded place like a public park and block out everything you hear but the sound of birds.

When you're back in the company of others, begin paying attention to how often you drift and daydream while others are speaking. Challenge yourself to come back to the current conversation. By working on the discipline of concentration in situations that aren't stressful, you will increase your ability to rely on it when you're standing in front of others and your adrenaline is off the charts.

Chapter Summary

The process of strengthening your mind allows you to combat distracting and interfering thoughts. When speaking, you're bombarded with hundreds of bits of nonsensical information, everything from "I have sweat running down my back" to "What a cute outfit" to "That person looks bored."

You have to ignore it all. You have to get in the zone. All performance is one part talent, one part skill, and two parts concentration. You simply have to ignore distractions and concentrate. Now that's a fine art worth mastering.

Chapter Seven:

Ten Thousand Hours and the Ninja Approach to Public Speaking

The art of speaking is like the art of music. Only after cords and foundations are well ingrained can jazz be made.
- Onlee Bowden

A long time ago, two days a week for about nine years, I studied martial arts. I am a black belt, first don, in a traditional Korean style called Tang Soo Do Moo Duk Kwan.

During the time I was training in the martial arts, I was also working on my master's degree at Central Michigan University and teaching public speaking. As a new teacher, my thoughts often drifted onto the topic of making communication come to life for my students. I wondered how I could make public speaking more exciting and realistic, and many of the answers came from my lessons in the dojo.

The beginning of each class started with floor drills. For about thirty minutes, we worked on strikes and blocks while our instructor came around to adjust and fine tune. We did these drills thousands of times, discovering the nuances of timing, strength, balance, and concentration.

I remember thinking that these moves were so deeply burned into my cells and muscles that, if I ever needed them, my body would respond without conscious thought. This was a good feeling, because knowing I could trust my body inspired real confidence.

That's when it struck me that this was the missing link in public speaking. Students needed a short list of physical skills they could practice every day until they could perform them naturally without conscious thought.

That's what sports training is about. A set of drills, patterns, and stances that impart maximum concentration, confidence, and impact. When your body is experiencing large surges of adrenaline and still performs, that's confidence you can rely on.

Athletes thrive when they use mind-body discipline to perform under pressure, and the same holds true with public speaking. There is a clear formula that works when teaching public speaking. It goes like this: clear teaching, forward-moving feedback, and a safe environment in which to practice. Training, practice, adjustment, training, fine tuning, and more practice.

The book Outliers by Malcolm Gladwell talks about an achievement concept called ten thousand hours. That's how long he believes it takes to attain mastery of any type of performance, whether it's music, art, math, or speaking. Gladwell anchors his claim on a multi-year study that followed a group of children who attended a school for the arts. All the children were either "very good" or actual prodigies; the hypothesis was that the prodigies would consistently outperform the "very good" students.

Surprisingly, the study revealed that mastery was not necessarily only for those with innate talent but rather was linked to how often the child practiced and continued to learn. Over the ten-year span, many children classified as "very good" outperformed the prodigies. It boiled down to training and practice.

Ten thousand hours is a long time. Mastering most skills does require this kind of focused commitment, but fortunately, speaking is a bit different. Since we already spend the majority of each day communicating, we can work on the core skills related to public speaking as much as we choose.

Over the next several chapters, you will be taught everything you need to know about public speaking. It won't take long, and you can begin practicing immediately. The rub is, you have to be your own taskmaster. (If you're reading this book with a group, please stop and decide who is going to be your speaking buddy. Yup, just like a training buddy with whom you make a promise of accountability.)

Chapter Summary

How freeing to know that, with mindful practice, we can master the core skills related to effective public speaking. They aren't a mystery, and becoming a comfortable and effective public speaker is truly attainable. We just have to put the time in and practice, practice, practice.

Chapter Eight:

The Four Levels of Learning

*Learning always throws the best parties. She laughs out loud
when Honesty and Brave start dancing.*
- Onlee Bowden

Often, when working on a set of skills that incorporate physical/body practices, we feel awkward and generally hyper aware. Have you ever taken a golf lesson and had your game actually get worse? It's this theory in practice.

The work in this chapter is credited to Abraham Maslow and Gordon Training International, among others; it can also be traced back to historical Eastern teachers. I use this model to help clients understand how they evolve through the process of learning the foundations of public speaking.

Each of the following levels provides insight into how we learn and why learning new skills can sometimes be hard work.

Level One: Unconscious Incompetence – You Don't Know What You Don't Know

Let's say you decide you want to learn how to weave. However, you're not sure where to start or even what you need to acquire.

You are unconsciously incompetent. You literally don't know what you don't know.

Level Two: Conscious Incompetence – Discovery

You do some reading and discover an art teacher from the local college who can teach you. You sign up, procure a supplies list, and buy what you need. You still don't know how to weave, but you are cognizant of the basics.

Level Three: Conscious Competence – The Rubber Hits the Road

You show up for class all excited, but you soon realize that weaving is harder than you imagined. You feel like you're all thumbs, and you begin to doubt if you will ever get good at this. What your instructor can accomplish in ten minutes, you can't do after three hours. Your back hurts from sitting so straight, and you're exhausted from concentrating so hard. Your teacher continually adjusts your technique, making you feel frustrated and overwhelmed.

The next week, you're slightly better, and you're even better the following week. After sixteen weeks, you're no pro, but you know that if you put your time in, you can actually weave and see results.

Level Four: Unconscious Competence – Muscle Memory and Transformation

You continue to weave after your class ends. The following spring, you discover yourself weaving to relax. You like to listen to music while letting your hands do what they seem to know how to do instinctively. You're no longer hyper-focused on the nuances of weaving, your back feels just fine, and your work is becoming a piece of art. Your life begins to feel more enriched, changed, and bigger.

Beyond Level Three and into Level Four

This course operates at level three with the goal of getting you to function at level four. Level three is hard work, and it's not uncommon to vacillate between levels three and four for a long time. Level three is where most of us feel uncomfortable because of the intense focus on the physical side of speaking.

It's a completely human tendency to shy away from doing things that make us feel awkward. That's why I call level three "the rubber hitting the road." All the hard work begins here, and no one can make you try except you. All I can tell you is that the more you do it, the better you will become.

All the skills I present are rooted in one absolute: your number one job is to get and keep your audience's attention. To get and keep attention is a lot of work. At any given point in your presentation, someone is surely drifting or daydreaming. Thus, the question is this: are you controlling the focus of your audience's eyes?

It's an interesting fact that where your eyes go, your thoughts follow. Are you walking all over, waving your notes, or playing with something? If so, you are in fact creating your largest distraction.

Are your points hard to follow? Do your ideas seem disconnected or merge into one continuous run-on sentence? These are also reasons people become distracted during presentations.

It's important to note that I'm teaching skills that professional speakers don't always demonstrate. I know many professional speakers who walk all over the stage, put their hands in their pockets, and let their arms fly.

There's no easy way to say this, so I'll just lay it on the line: you're not them. You don't have a crew behind you working with lights, music, and images. You don't travel around speaking on only one or two well-crafted topics. You're not Mark Zuckerberg, Oprah, or the Dalai Lama, and you haven't written the latest bestseller.

You're just you. You speak from time to time while you work your day job, so you need to learn the foundations of effective public speaking.

Level four competency is absolutely attainable for everyone willing to put the time in. Now when I speak, my body is at level four and it takes care of me, freeing me to concentrate on the message and my audience. I never feel like my body is out of control, and all those emotional triggers that used to plague my thoughts are actually gone. I have deep confidence in my body when I'm presenting in front of others, and this is an amazing place to be.

Chapter Summary

Don't skip or cherry pick from the foundation, or you're likely to miss the very transformation you're seeking. Level three is hard, awkward work, and there's no way around it, only through it.

However, the true goal is to achieve level four, or muscle memory. I want your body to take care of you when you speak, not the other way around. If you are willing to practice through level three, you will gain the reward of level four competency. This means your body will monitor your anxiety and effectively diffuse it by doing what it has been trained to do. Your negative self-talk will diminish and be replaced with a level four speaking recall model that keeps your ideas organized and moving forward.

Level four frees you up to be yourself, to find the humor, to really make your audience comfortable. In level four, you begin to discover the art in speaking as you learn how to use stories and examples to anchor your ideas.

I love level four, I really do, and I wish it for everyone.

Chapter Nine:

Break It Down

Yes loves to play outdoors and run through the streams barefoot.
She just wishes she could convince No to join her.
- Onlee Bowden

I t's time to settle the internal voice of fear and judgment for once and for all, so let's get started. If you feel yourself saying "No," say "Yes" instead. Trust in a better way of speaking. Trust yourself to learn. Give yourself permission to feel stupid, awkward, or clumsy. Give yourself permission to try and try again until it feels just right. Give yourself permission to expand, and tell your family and friends to give you some space as you work on your stuff.

Your Body Is the Springboard for Calm and Energized

You, your body, your being, your essence, is your platform. Like it or not, people are looking at you when you stand up to speak. What people remember about you and your message can only be conveyed through your platform. That's why we are going to work from the ground up, starting with your stance and ending with your face.

70/30 Stance and Spanx!

Everything starts with your stance. Your aim is to have your feet solidly under your hips. Your shoulders should be relaxed and down below your ears. Focus on a long neck, a relaxed throat, and breathing from your diaphragm.

A solid stance means having a foundation that's balanced and strong yet resilient; this foundation serves the same purpose as Spanx, those comfortable undergarments that keep everything together, where you want it, yet flexible.

When speaking, many people stand with both feet forward. Don't do this! Standing with both feet forward is actually an unbalanced stance. If you were to think about where your center of gravity is while standing with both feet forward, it's vacillating between the balls of your feet and your heels.

Try it…Notice how you move backward and forward? You are definitely not balanced. Now shift your feet into a slight 45-degree angle with one foot slightly in front of the other. Better, huh?

Now look down. Are your feet more than shoulder width apart? If so, simply move them in a little. It doesn't matter which foot is forward; whichever feels the most comfortable is fine.

Now shift 70% of your weight to your back foot and 30% to your front foot. A good way to check if your weight distribution is 70/30 is to pick up the front foot. Do you have to shift your weight? If so, you're not quite there yet. Bring your feet together just a little more until you are.

Now make your knees spongy. Don't do any real bending; just unlock them. Keep both knees relaxed. We humans have a tendency to lock the back knee, and you'll know you're doing it if you feel your hip rise on that side.

Look in the mirror. Your stance should look very natural. If it doesn't, keep adjusting. Remember, a slight 45-degree angle, one foot slightly in front of the other, body weight 70% on the back foot and 30% on the front, and spongy knees.

Now you're balanced! Practice this every time you're standing, anywhere. Practice it all day! It doesn't take additional time; you simply need to be mindful about doing it. If it feels weird, keep doing it until you no longer have to think about it.

Should I Move around the Stage?

For most people and in most settings, I don't recommend moving around the stage. Here's why: we move to deal with the adrenal dump hitting our bodies. We try to walk it out, but it seldom works like that. Instead, the more we walk without purpose, the more nervous we appear.

The rule of thumb regarding walking is to ask yourself what your purpose is. Are you moving forward to your audience for a reason, such as to talk with a specific section of people, or are you moving just to move?

My Signature Move

We have a place in our brains that creates a balance between stress and relaxation. When this area of the brain is stimulated by either conscious or unconscious stress, it sends a signal to our adrenal glands, which are located just above the kidneys. Adrenaline acts on muscles by sending more blood to key muscle groups. Adrenaline gets our muscles ready to go. This is why people can experience superhuman strength when faced with an emergency.

At the same time that adrenaline primes our muscles to go, smaller muscles like our tendons contract, which means they shorten and tighten in order to prepare our bodies for extreme physical abilities. After all, that's what adrenaline is designed to do, activate our muscles for intense action.

Now let's think about public speaking. The amount of adrenaline we release when we're speaking is significant. It's enough to make our blood pressure rise, our heart rate increase, and to cause shaking, sweating, and a warped sense of time. It also distorts our memories, our perceptions, and our ability to recall information.

Ironically, while our bodies are preparing for extreme and intense action, the event called public speaking calls for the opposite. We must appear calm and relaxed in spite of the fact that all of our muscles are constricting.

Every muscle is constricting...Think about that. Your fingers, face, arms, legs, and chest muscles are all tightening. Just writing about it makes me feel a little panicky!

When we have a full-blown adrenal dump while speaking, we are physically out of control. We walk around, shove our hands into our pockets, play with our pens, hair, scarves, or notes, and walk around some more. Our hands constrict, so they shake; so do our legs, so they shake, too. These muscles need to relax. If they are tense, they shake.

There is only one muscle group large enough to handle adrenaline while allowing the rest of the body to relax, and this is the derriere…Yup, the gluteus maximus.

Don't believe me? Try squeezing your butt like there's no tomorrow. Then, during an adrenaline dump, see what happens when you squeeze anything other than your derrière. Squeeze your notes and they shake; tighten your legs and they shake. In fact, anywhere you hold tension will shake except your derriere.

To combat your adrenaline rush, find your 70/30 stance and relax your knees, arms, face, and throat. Relax your breathing and squeeze your butt. Take your hands out of your pockets and squeeze your butt. Stop walking around and squeeze your butt. Smile and squeeze, breathe and squeeze, relax everything except your derriere, and squeeze.

You can practice this any time. You don't need a gym membership, and you don't need to carve out time to do it. Every time you're standing, find your stance and squeeze. Actually, the more you practice, the quicker your body will respond and relax. Note: you can't simultaneously walk and squeeze; that's just weird.

Every person who has taken a class with me will vouch that this technique works. In an adrenal dump, your body is having a real physical phenomenon, and you can't just think it away. You have to combat physical with physical, and squeezing your butt like there's no tomorrow will give you control over your shaking.

If this doesn't work right away, keep doing it. More than likely, you're unconsciously holding tension in some other muscle group. Perhaps you're holding your notes too tightly. If so, they will shake. If your voice feels shaky, you're holding tension in your throat. If you're done speaking and you're out of breath, it's because you were holding your breath.

The Speaking Triangle

We are unconsciously drawn to faces; we have been since we were infants. This is where we glean our cues about how to feel or respond. We laugh when others laugh, we smile when others smile, and we cry when others cry.

I call this place where voices, facial expressions, and gestures come together to send one clear message the sweet zone. To get the most out of this zone, it's important to direct the eyes of your audience into what I call "the speaking triangle."

The speaking triangle is a simple concept that keeps your audience focused on your face and upper body, which is a natural point of focus for them. What happens when you have action going on below your waist? It forces audience members to divide their attention. After all, how can they watch your face when your hands are moving in your pockets? Likewise, if you're not using the 70/30 stance, you're probably moving around or swaying or crossing your feet. Think about what that's doing to your audience. With all this going on, how can their eyes be in the speaking triangle, watching your face?

Create the speaking triangle by bringing your hands above your head and touching your fingertips together. This begins the top of the triangle.

Now bring your hands down and out from the sides. Finally, bring them in to meet in the middle of your waist.

Note that this triangle expands as the room does. If you're in a small space, the triangle is small and intimate. If you're speaking at a podium, your triangle is larger and has to be bigger than the podium. If you're on a stage, your triangle is even larger in order to compensate for the distance between you and your audience.

Everything needs to stay inside the speaking triangle. Remember, the goal is to get and keep the attention of your audience. When there's something going on outside the triangle, it divides your audience's attention. If your hand is to your side and gesturing, it forces the audience to decide what to watch. Bring your hand up and into the triangle; it wants to be in the game, and it's trying to tell you this.

If the triangle is the sweet zone, what exactly happens there? Let's take a closer look inside this area.

Holding Notes

Consider your notes to be a professional extension of your professional self. They need to look and function at that level. You will either be speaking from an electronic tablet using the speaking wheel or you will make a printed copy and use this for your notes. Either way, how you handle your notes speaks volumes, so getting it right matters.

Here are a few tips for effectively managing your speaking notes:

•   If you print your speaking wheel, use regular-sized legal paper. You need visual space on your paper in order to find what's there fast. Small notepads and note cards do not allow for empty space between words. We look down at notes quickly with adrenaline soaring through our bodies, so images or words written too small will blur together.

•   Put your notes on a legal pad that has a solid back. Never, ever hold a piece of paper without a solid back. On the other hand, don't hold a five-pound super notebook either. Too flimsy or too heavy will force you to hold your notes tightly, constricting those muscles.

•   Our non-dominant hand seems to wander a lot during speeches. This is the hand searching for a place to land. It needs a job, so forevermore make it your official note holder. This hand needs to remain relaxed and calm, yet at your waist. For more control without creating tension, hold notes from the side, not the bottom. Spread your fingers out under the notepad or tablet to create a steadier platform and let your thumb rest softly on the front. This allows your dominant hand, the power hand, to do all the gesturing. Avoid letting your non-dominant hand gesture so much that your notes move and create a distraction.

- Notes anchor one side of the speaking triangle and are held a little off center, keeping your body open to your audience. Your notes are only for you, and they need to be there at a moment's notice. If your notes are down, clutched to your chest, or flopped over, they are no longer working for you.

- Always think of your notes as a professional extension of yourself. A clean legal pad or tablet held professionally is the goal. If holding notes feels uncomfortable and you want to put them down, don't. Remember, you're working on level three, becoming consciously competent. Level three is often awkward until you do it for a while. Walk around the office holding a legal pad. This isn't hard to do, so just incorporate it into your day. Put a legal pad in your non-dominant hand, slightly over the side of your body, and get used to not moving it. It won't be long until it will go there naturally...level four!

Gestures

When should you gesture? How many is too many? What's the best gesture? Is it the point, the two-fingered point, the closed fist, the fist-hit into the other hand, the fist-hit on the podium, or the speak-to-the-hand gesture? Or is it fingers tight together, fingers all flappy like a butterfly, or maybe the Baptist opened-armed V?

Whoa. Enough already. Too much time is spent deciphering the meaning behind the elusive gesture and trying to get it just right.

Here's my read on this: only two things really matter. First, all gestures should be above the waist and in the speaking triangle. Second, gestures have a beginning and an end.

Gestures are best when they start and stop. By allowing your gestures to stop and rest, you allow your audience to absorb information more easily. You can also slow down how fast your mind is racing by slowing down your gestures. Watch a child who is all excited about something. Watch this child's hands. They're moving about a hundred miles an hour, and so is the child's brain. We usually say, "Okay, let's slow down," and we demonstrate by slowing down our own hands. This is calming and reassuring, and it helps maintain focus.

The same holds true for us as speakers. The pace of our gestures adds to our overall sense of calm or anxiety and can slow down or speed up our central nervous system. If we feel like we are soaring through our presentation, we can actually slow it down by slowing down our gestures. By slowing down our gestures, we also slow our thinking patterns down. Many presenters express feeling that time is moving faster than normal, and there is something to that. Adrenaline speeds up our thinking process and makes it hard sometimes to catch up with it, leaving us at a loss for words. By squeezing, relaxing, breathing, and slowing down our gestures, we create a feedback loop that tells our bodies to relax, thus allowing our thoughts to become clearer.

Eye Contact

It's so true…We manage our audience through our eye contact. If you want your audience's attention, look at them. Not over them, or on the floor, or over their shoulders – at them. The more you look at your audience, the more focused they will be on you.

I teach people to look at an audience member for about the count of "one-one thousand, two-one thousand" before moving on. The key is to move your eye contact around so those sitting close or those sitting farther away feel included. You can improve your eye contact by working on it every day. You already know if this is an issue for you. If it is, it's time to get a handle on it.

Weirdly enough, this is one of the areas I work on. Basically, I have a reoccurring habit of looking over people's shoulders when I speak with them. Occasionally, I actually have people look over their own shoulder, trying to see what I am looking at, in the middle of a conversation. How embarrassing! I've actually had friends tell me to look at them more. Yikes…

To improve, I first needed to develop awareness of this problem and then make conscious changes. I discovered I look away the most when I'm telling a story. I think sometimes I'm imagining the story as I tell it, and that's what I'm looking at. Other times, I look away trying to find a word or idea. The problem is, once I look away, I have a tendency to stay there. To improve, I work on looking more directly at people when I'm telling stories and when I'm trying to remember something. It takes work, and I'll admit, I'm better when I work on it.

Eye contact really is important to your audience. It's so easy to drift and daydream while others are talking, and we all fall victim to it. If my goal is to get and keep my audience's attention, I need to make eye contact with many audience members, and often. It greatly reduces their tendency to drift and daydream.

We may not want to be "called out" in an audience, but we do like making eye contact with the speaker. It makes us feel a part of the experience, kind of special, and we usually remember such experiences as stand-out moments. I remember once going to a Paul Simon, Rhythm of the Saints concert with a friend. Our seats were front right of stage, and at one point, Paul Simon looked directly at my friend and smiled. That was it...

Build an Internal Compass – Practice in Front of a Mirror

Since level four is unconscious competence or muscle memory, it is critical to develop muscle memory. To move from level three to four requires developing a new sense of body awareness. If you practice the following skill sets in front of a mirror, you can begin to align what you're doing physically with the muscle groups that are being activated internally. Mirror work is designed to get us more in tune with our bodies when we are performing. The best indicator of how we're doing ultimately needs to come from within.

Learn to feel the muscles in your face as you smile. Learn to read your body quickly and without judgment, and then use this information to make quick adjustments. If you're rocking, it's just feedback telling your body to find your speaking stance, relax, and squeeze. If you see your notes moving all over, stop, relax, and squeeze. If your gestures are moving too fast, acknowledge this and slow them down. Are your hands gesturing by your side? No problem; they're just trying to tell you to bring them up and let them be in the speaking triangle. Over time, your brain and your body will find a way to talk back and forth. This is called bio-feedback.

Check Your Stance and Speaking Notes

Stand in front of a mirror, get into your speaking stance, and hold your notes. Take a good look and then close your eyes. What does your body feel like when you're in the stance? What muscles are being used? What feels relaxed? How is your breathing? How about your notes? Can you feel them slightly to your side? Are your notes upright or bending forward? Is your arm relaxed, or does it feel tense?

Open your eyes and check how things look. Make any necessary adjustments. Now close your eyes again, move around, and then come back to the stance with your eyes closed.

Now open your eyes and check your body. Are your feet in the 70/30 stance? Are your hands in the speaking triangle? Where are your notes? How are you holding them? As needed, adjust your stance, hands, or notepad and keep going.

Check Your Facial Expressions

Mirror work is excellent for helping us understand how the muscles in our faces work. Remember, adrenaline constricts our muscles, which means our faces have to work twice as hard to appear relaxed and open.

Take a good look at your face. Now let it go to its neutral position. This is what you look like when you're not conscious. Most neutral faces looked bored or angry. How does yours look?

Now raise your eyebrows and use your eyes to smile. Feel the different muscles being used to raise your eyebrows. Feel the muscles in your face when you smile. Is your face warm and inviting? Do you smile warmly with your eyes? Work on this until it becomes natural for you to look warm and inviting.

Check Your Gestures

Watch your gestures in the mirror. Are they confident and complete? Do they stay inside the speaking triangle?

Now let your hands rest comfortably by your side. Watch your hands and fingers. Are they twitching? If so, take a breath in, let it go, squeeze your butt, and relax your fingers. A twitch is just feedback telling your body to take action. The more you notice and adjust during mirror work, the faster your body will respond in other, more stressful, settings.

If you commit to practicing these techniques five minutes a day over the next few weeks, you won't believe the arsenal of skills you'll develop.

Chapter Summary

The skills presented in this chapter can be acquired by anyone, which means you absolutely can become a stronger, more effective public speaker. Learn the stance and squeeze those buns. Pay attention to the speaking triangle and how you hold your notes, how you gesture, and how you make eye contact. Practice in front of the mirror. Become aware of your facial expressions. Internalize it all. Good public speaking skills are yours for the taking, little Ninja.

Chapter Ten:

Structure Is Freedom, Part 1
(Intros and Conclusions)

Creativity without her friend Structure is a hot mess.
- Onlee Bowden

I'm a seventies child. Born in 1958, I grew up with The Addams Family, cars without seatbelts, big wide bellbottoms, sneaking into restaurants without shoes, and a deep-seated belief in life, love, and the pursuit of happiness.

The word "goal" was nowhere in my vocabulary. In fact, whenever someone started talking about goals, I mentally turned the station.

Luckily, now that I'm older, smarter, and hopefully more mature, I have a very different perspective on what freedom really means. However, I'm still me, and I don't want to feel too confined. They say opposites attract, and this holds true in my life.

Recently, my husband and I decided to take Dave Ramsey's Financial Peace seminar. In lesson two, Ramsey talked about how each marriage has a nerd spirit and a free spirit. Well, I married a CPA, so I think you can quickly deduce which of the two descriptions fits me. In fact, I tell people I "married into math." I say this to emphasize how hard it was for me, a free spirit, to not only learn the worth of structure but to advocate that structure actually provides freedom when speaking in public.

In my studio classes, we spend the first session just talking about public speaking. People share that they often lose sleep trying to figure out what should go into a presentation. In our last class, I do a check-in and compare where they are now with how they started.

Clients consistently express a great sense of freedom at having a simple structure that allows them to easily put together a presentation, and I never fail to feel amazed at how a simple structure can make such a difference. I now "get" how structure can enable freedom.

When speakers have a road map for moving through a presentation and know what's going to come first, second, and third, they experience a tremendous shift in confidence. They develop the ability to move in and out of stories and examples without becoming lost. If they ever do get lost, they still don't have to worry, because they have a map to follow based on eye/brain recognition. Without this roadmap, here's how presentations often play out:

You are making a presentation. You speak for a while without referring to your notes, and then something breaks your concentration. You lose your place, so your eyes automatically begin to scan your notes. This instantly creates a marked increase in adrenaline in your body. As a result, your notes become blurry. You look top to bottom, confused. Where is it? The information you need was there when you practiced, but you can't find it now! Seconds feel like minutes, and sometimes they do turn into minutes as you try to pull a rabbit out of a hat from somewhere in the middle.

Have you ever gotten lost when speaking in public? What happened when you couldn't find a key idea in your notes? This experience is without a doubt one of the worst that can occur in a presentation. Once they've given up trying to find where they were, most people just wing it, but filmmaker Michael Bay actually walked off stage during a live appearance after his teleprompter failed, too confounded to regroup.

This issue is so significant that, for years, I kept going back to the problem in search of a solution. When I was teaching public speaking at Central Michigan University, I told students that successful speeches actually go full circle, with the ending referring back to the beginning, yet even then I realized this didn't jive with the typical method of utilizing notes from top to bottom.

About this same time, I was introduced to Tony Buzan's book Mind Mapping and discovered how he used circles for creative problem solving. He also talked about eye/brain recognition and how our brains recognize colors over black and white, our own printing over typed words, and images over words. These beginnings were the portal to my own design called the Bowden Speaking Wheel.

If you open any public speaking textbook or purchase an app for speaking notes, you will quickly discover that all speech structures are set up top to bottom. I.e., the introduction is at the top of the page, the body comes in the middle, and the closing comes at the bottom. We all learned to speak using this method of top-to-bottom speaking notes.

Physically, if you are using notes, this means that as you present, your eyes must continually scan the page for the next spot in the presentation. If you're using a speaking app, you must constantly scroll with your finger to the next spot, relying on your ability to remember the sequence of your speech because it's not in front of you in its entirety.

All traditional organizational schemes use a linear approach to structure. In fact, we've done this for so long and are so used to it that we're mostly blind to it. However, what if this very structure is in fact the single most compelling reason people experience speech anxiety?

The Bowden Speaking Wheel is designed to keep the entire presentation in front of you the entire time you're speaking. It also anchors your presentation at a glance, automatically directing your eyes to the correct spot with no scanning required.

Clocks Are the Perfect Mate

Earlier, I argued that we cannot expect to be perfect speakers because communication is inherently messy. I'm still waving that flag, but it doesn't mean we can't be armed with crazy-great tools.

In fact, we need a speaking tool that takes no extra brain power to use. It must be easy to visualize, so it seemed natural to call upon an image we already have in our collective memory banks – the clock. Yes, the ordinary, almost obsolete, clock.

It's easy to visualize a clock. We don't have to work to see it. We can also imagine numbers on a clock without any effort, so I decided to design a presentation around this familiar image using an easily recognized circle with set points at 12, 3, 6, and 9. This structure could anchor any presentation, I decided, and thus the clock became my model for an organized, fluent, eye-friendly speech.

The Bowden Speaking Wheel Unpacked, Intros and Conclusions

Now let's create the speaking wheel that allows you to come full circle in your presentations. Take a piece of paper and draw a circle about the size a healthy soup bowl. On the outside of the circle, write the numbers 12, 3, 6, and 9 in their correct spots on the clock.

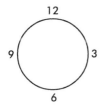

Now draw a line between 3 and 9. This will cut your circle horizontally in half.

Now draw a parallel line from 12 until it meets the horizontal line in the middle of the circle. This will create three sections, with the bottom section the largest.

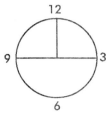

What you now have are the three pieces, or movements, that all presentations have: the introduction, the body, and the conclusion. Think of it this way: you gotta get in, say something, and get out.

12:00 through 3:00: The Introduction, or "You Gotta Get In"

Successful introductions are carefully structured to capture as many audience members as possible in a short amount of time. It's sort of like the irresistible sirens in the movie O Brother, Where Art Thou? Everett, Pete, and Delmar were helpless against the sirens because each of them heard exactly what he needed and wanted to hear.

The same holds true with good introductions, which if done right irresistibly pull people in. Imagine that the introduction is designed like a funnel, wide at the top and narrow toward the bottom. Being wide at the top allows maximum flexibility when choosing the best attention-getter for the audience. A narrow bottom creates a lazar sharp focus on the topic and main points.

Now go back to your clock. Add the numbers 1 and 2 to your circle where they naturally belong. The 12 is your attention getter, 1 is the reaction to the attention getter, 2 is the big idea, also called the title of the speech, and 3 is the preview of your main points. This area from 12 to 3 is now and forever your introduction.

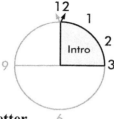

12:00: The Attention Getter

A classic blunder many speakers make is deciding not to use an attention getter. Without an attention getter, you derail your own presentation because your audience has to quickly focus on the topic without any context. Again, remember the funnel; it's wide at the top and quickly narrows at the bottom, allowing the contents to flow smoothly.

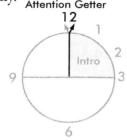

Let's look at which attention getter works best. I highly recommend the short story. Having been in this business since

1982, I've listened to and given feedback on over sixteen thousand speeches, so trust me when I say the safest, most effective, and most trustworthy way to begin a speech is with a quick story.

It's easier to begin with a story than with other attention getters. In addition, when speakers tell a story, they immediately calm down. The effective attention-getting story is one that sheds light on the topic without giving too much away. It can be your story, his story, the neighbors' story, something you read, or something from the news; just give credit where credit is due and tell the story.

It's far easier to remember a story than a quote or statistics, and it's safer to tell a story than to tell a joke. Quotes and numbers have to be exact, which creates a higher level of stress for you, and jokes often unexpectedly fall flat or inadvertently offend.

Your attention getter plays two important roles in your presentation. First, it sparks an interest in your topic. Second, it provides a way for your audience to connect into the essence, the feel, of your presentation. All presentations carry a rhythm or a feel about them, and this is set by you, the presenter, so slow down and enjoy the story you're about to tell.

1:00: React to Your Own Attention Getter

I added this piece after watching speakers complete a really good attention getter and then just stop, unsure of how to move forward. How do you tie your story into the presentation that follows?

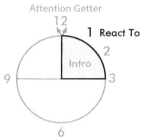

You chose that particular attention getter for a reason. What was it? Why did you pick that story? How does that story make you feel when you hear it? What have you gleaned from the story?

Share this with your audience. It will sound something like this: "When I first heard/read that story, my world just stopped for a moment." Or, "When I look back on that moment, I realized...."

What you're doing is sharing your own reactions with the audience. You're taking your audience down the same path you traveled when you first heard or experienced this story. This is a good way to build credibility with your audience, and it provides a smooth transition into the next part of your speech. As you react, you can explain your relationship to the topic, such as, "As a mother of two daughters, I could relate to how she was feeling."

2:00: State the Big Idea

Every single presentation is based on one really big idea. Think of this as the title of your presentation. Let's say you're asked to give a presentation on reducing debt for American families. Your big idea, and your title, is "reducing debt for American families."

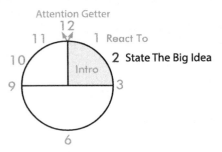

You now need to build a presentation around the title, but beware: although it's the title of the speech, you don't begin with it. You start with the attention getter, you then react to your attention getter, and only then do you state the big idea.

Inexperienced speakers will begin by saying something like, "My topic today is reducing debt for American families." They will skip right over the attention getter and go right to the meat. They will justify this all day long with comments like, "Well, I don't want to bore my audience with trivial stuff, so I just get to it."

The real truth sounds something more like this: "Well, I'm not very good at starting a presentation, so I just get right to it."

When you don't start with an attention getter, your audience must scramble to mentally catch up. Why? Because they are not tuned in yet.

Likewise, when you fail to respond to your own attention getter, you create an awkward moment that both you and your audience must recover from.

Get good at handling these first steps of your introduction. Trust me; it will pay off. Only then do you move into the big idea, which you state in one clean sentence such as the following: "Today I want to talk about reducing debt for American families."

3:00: Preview the Main Points

Before you dive into your presentation, briefly tell your audience what you're going to cover. This will put your audience at ease and help them concentrate better. Remember, your number one goal is to get and keep your audience's attention; you do this by keeping them in the loop regarding where the presentation is going.

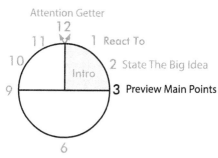

Every big idea can go in hundreds of directions, so you need to narrow the scope. Your preview will sound something like this: "Today, I'm going to talk about reducing debt for American families [the big idea]. That's a big topic, so I'm going to focus on three areas [the preview]: first, the myth of credit, second, the freedom of being debt free, and third, living a debt-free lifestyle."

First, second, third…That's how it's done. You tell your audience exactly where the presentation is going. It's that clean and that simple. At this time, only preview the main points; do not preview the details inside the main points.

Your structure should always be simple, transparent, and spoken out loud. Do not confuse this structure for speaking with writing. In writing, structure can be more subtle, more behind the scenes, but not so with public speaking. The audience listening to a presentation gets only one chance to follow the presentation. Unless it's recorded, audiences must depend on the speaker to communicate the structure.

Be overt in your communication of structure because it gives you instant credibility. Without structure, a presentation is simply a string of thoughts with no beginning and no end. Previewing and reviewing your ideas gains you the attention and respect of others. It compels your audience to think, "Okay, good; she is going to cover these areas."

As an aside, bosses really appreciate it, too!

9:00 through 12:00: The Conclusion

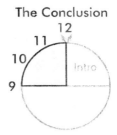

The Conclusion

An effective conclusion is way more than just the home stretch, and it requires as much forethought as the introduction. Alas, otherwise effective presentations often deteriorate, as the following scenario demonstrates:

You're speaking, and you've given it your all. You got a little lost here and there, but it was no big deal because you were using the speaking circle. People laughed at your stories, and at one point someone actually said, "Aww."

You are rounding the circle and heading into the home stretch, feeling good, when you see it – the light at the end of the tunnel.

Suddenly, you begin to sprint. What did you just say? You don't know because the light is so shiny. You mumble something that sounds suspiciously redundant. Your brain is screaming, "Get out; get out now!" so you offer a rushed "Thank you" and walk away feeling awkward and even embarrassed.

There's no way around the truth: in your eagerness to be done, you flubbed the ending.

I've seen this so many times, the solid speech that ends sideways. We fallible human beings tend to go over and over the beginning and body of the speech and then forget about the ending. We need to remember that it's not over till it's over.

The cool thing is that successful conclusions practically mirror their introductions. Here's how you go about developing an effective conclusion.

9:00: Review the Main Points (Part One of Your Conclusion)

If 3:00 is the preview, 9:00 is the review. This is where you begin wrapping things up, and you do this by telling your audience what you told them.

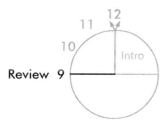

Yup, you do it one more time. A review of your main points is one clean sentence that goes something like this: "So today I talked about three areas, the myth of credit, the freedom of being debt free, and living a debt-free lifestyle."

10:00: Restate the Big Idea (Part Two of Your Conclusion)

Look across the speaking circle, and you'll see 2:00, State the Big Idea. Not surprisingly, 10:00 simply restates the big idea. In so doing, it reinforces the heart of why you spoke.

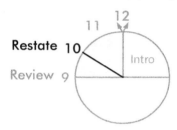

I get to 10:00 by tying it into my review. It sounds like this: "So today I talked about three areas; the myth of credit, the freedom of being debt free, and living a debt-free lifestyle [review of main points]. Why did I talk about this? Because reducing debt for American families [the big idea] is critical to our future."

It's as simple as that.

11:00: Bring the Attention Getter Full Circle (Part Three of Your Conclusion)

When a speech goes full circle, it comes right back to how it began by touching on the attention getter. When you bring your presentation full circle in this way, people will be impressed.

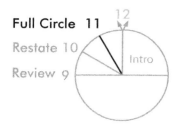

Full Circle 11
Restate 10
Review 9
Intro
12

Most will have forgotten about the attention getter, and when you come back to it, refreshing their memories, it's fitting and clever and it makes a presentation feel well rounded.

Sometimes I refer to eleven o'clock as "kissing the attention getter." By kissing the attention getter, you're evoking a feeling of unity, which makes your audience feel well cared for.

How you get back to your attention getter varies. Here are some tried-and-true methods:

• You can weigh in on your attention getter by saying something like this: "I think Bebe Hogan was brave when she refused to stand in line."

• You can remind us how you felt when you heard the story you shared in the attention getter with something like this: "It still breaks my heart when I think about those children hiding for six days."

• You can use cliffhangers as attention-getting stories and then come back and tell the rest of the story at eleven o'clock: "Remember Drew, who was hanging off the side of the mountain with frost bite? Here's what happened…" The key is, come back to it. Don't pass over this very memorable gem.

12:00: End with Impact (Part Four of Your Conclusion)

To end with impact, turn the presentation over to your audience and give them something to chew on. This is the time to offer up a quote, a poem, or a challenge.

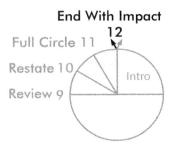

End With Impact

Ending with impact will sound something like this: "As you leave today, consider the words of Albert Einstein: 'Imagination is more important than knowledge.' Here's a genius pointing us away from rote learning and toward creativity. I believe he is challenging every teacher to reconsider not only how they teach but also what is being taught."

I usually say something like, "As you leave today," or "I want to leave you with this…"

Ending with impact is about sounding like you're ending. It incorporates timing and tone. It's strong, sure, and definite. To do it well, slow your words, make solid eye contact, and smile.

Never, ever give up on your ending. If the last words out of your mouth don't sound like an ending, say one more thing that does. Remember the toast scene in the movie Bridesmaids when two of the bridesmaids fight over who will have the last word?

The last word is important. Don't squander it. I know the light is there, begging you to run toward it, but it's not your time. Resist, Pilgrim!

Chapter Summary

I started by saying that structure is freedom, and I want to end with the same sentiment. The feeling of freedom that comes from knowing what you want to say first, second, and third is amazing, and it leads to true confidence.

The Speaking Wheel

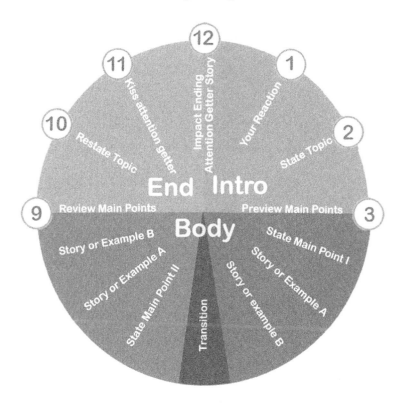

Chapter Eleven:

Structure Is Freedom, Part 2
(Main Points and the Use of Stories)

Structure without Creativity does her laundry every
Saturday night, pronto.
- Onlee Bowden

The meat of your presentation is called the body. This is where the big idea comes to life. It's the heart and soul of any presentation. Now is your time to really say something, so what are you going to focus on and how much are you going to say?

What you're going to talk about can create a great deal of worry. Oftentimes, this is where fear gets involved. We worry about how much to cover and how to make it optimally useful for our audience. These are valid concerns and they need to be addressed, but how? What are the best decisions concerning the body of your speech?

The most memorable and perhaps the most influential presentations usually combine credible fact with credible emotion. It can be argued that all presentations have a persuasive element, from a new approach to a gentle reminder to an all-out call for action. All presentations are designed to move your audience in some way. To help reduce the struggle, consider the following guidelines when designing your message:

• No more than three main points for any speech. When you start to put four, five, and six main points into a presentation, you're setting yourself up for failure. Audiences are liable to become impatient at three main points, and more than three is simply too much to handle.

Based on who your audience is, pick the top three most important pieces to share. If there seem to be more than three main points, I suggest a reexamination. Can you consolidate information into three chunks? Perhaps you can use an organizing scheme for your three main points. For example, maybe main point one presents the problem, main point two presents the solution, and main point three presents what's needed next. This approach of problem, solution, and what's next is called an organizing theme. Organizing themes can be any combination of two or three points that build in some logical form.

A few weeks back, a client asked me to help design a presentation for her employees. After some conversation about why this was important right now to her crew, we analyzed what makes her organization tick. We landed on this theme/topic/title: "We do Inventive and Guts Better Than Anyone."

The three main points are these: 1. the past, 2. the present, and 3. the future. All three points were about her crew's innovation and guts to keep pushing forward but from three perspectives, past, present, and future.

If you have more points that you consider essential and you can't fit them in by restructuring your information, consider providing that information in handouts at the end; simply tell your audience you're providing more information on the topics after the presentation.

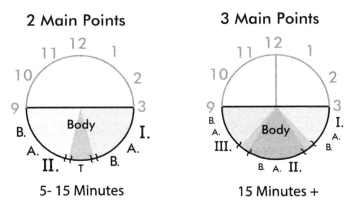

2 Main Points
5- 15 Minutes

3 Main Points
15 Minutes +

• The number of main points is determined by the amount of time you have to speak. Fifteen minutes allows time for three main points. Fewer than fifteen minutes allows for two main points. The more time you have, the more in depth you can go. If you're speaking for fifty minutes, you will still present three main points with ample time to develop them.

• Be sure to use a mix of emotional and logical appeals when speaking. People want both when making a decision. Emotional appeals hit them in the heart, while logical appeals hit them in the brain. Don't leave either out.

- Once you preview your main points, you must talk about them. If you run out of time and leave a main point out, your audience will have no choice but to conclude you didn't manage your time well. This is one of many reasons it's wise to develop no more than two or three main points.

- When speaking, time moves fast, so consider how much time you will spend with each main point, and always keep a clock directly in front of you to manage your time. Most of us are asked to speak somewhere between ten and fifty minutes. Divide your presentation time using the following ratio: introduction 25%, body 50%, and conclusion 25%.

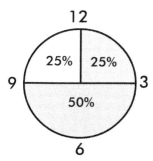

By the way, do not expect to find a clock these days in boardrooms or conference rooms. They just aren't there, so always take something you can keep an eye on. Whatever you use, it needs to be at-a-glance available. Don't check your watch or pull out your phone; this is clumsy and obvious. Instead, watching your time throughout the presentation will let you ebb and flow as needed. If you only check your time occasionally, you're very likely to be surprised at how much has passed.

- With respect to time, never say anything like, "Oh wow, my time has gotten away from me." Likewise, don't get frazzled about time. Keep it to yourself. Later in this chapter, under the section titled "Editing during Your Presentation," I'll explain just how easy it is to manage your time when following the methods in this book.

• When making a case for change or action, be sure to back up your ideas with the work and respected opinions of others in the field. Legitimate opinions are important. Again, it all goes back to knowing who your audience is. We now have so much information at our fingertips that we're expected to use the most up-to-date information offered by the most credible sources.

Once I took my daughter to a dermatologist who told me chocolate did not lead to complexion issues and that this was backed by research. I asked who funded the research and was told "Hershey's."

Exactly.

This is why you always need to check how information was gathered and who conducted the research; also check to see who funded the research. You might be surprised.

When citing a source, be sure to mention it first and present the actual work second. The same is true when you're quoting someone. Tell whom you're quoting first and then give the quote. It will sound something like this: "Yesterday, I caught a story about Tillie Rayburn and her unwavering courage when she ran back into a burning building in Chicago. I was impressed with her sense of calm; let me read what she said."

- Any time you use numbers, statistics, or quotes, employ one of two strategies.

Strategy one is to use visuals, but let me emphasize that you are to use visuals, not kill your audience with them. Only use visuals to enhance the message. Avoid at all costs developing a PowerPoint presentation that simply reflects your structure.

Be creative with visuals because that's what they are, visuals. Use them to give depth, to highlight, or to make a concept clearer. Images are amazing for creating a lasting memory for your audience, and the more competent you become at incorporating technology into your presentations, the more your audience will be drawn in.

However, always be prepared for technical problems. My rule is to prepare all presentations with the expectation that the technical side will fail. I'm serious; always plan for the "What if" moment whenever you use something technical. I've watched far too many presenters mess with their computers up to and actually during their presentations. Always be prepared to deliver a presentation with no technical support whatsoever.

Strategy two is to simply to tell your audience that you're going to read to them. It will sound something like this: "Last month, the CDC released some surprising information. I want to read these results to you." Or, "Harper Range was quoted in The Savage saying the following; let me read this to you."

Why do I advocate telling your audience you're going to read something to them? First, if the information you're sharing is new to you, the odds of forgetting details are high. You can avoid this awkward moment by telling your audience that you're going to read. By doing this, you appear seamless rather than unsure or lost. Second, when you're reading, you separate yourself just enough from the information to inject your own reaction.

Reading also allows you to slow the pace down and actually repeat pieces for emphasis or even take the time to mindfully control your voice if it's shaking just the slightest bit.

Quotes, numbers, and images are punctuated moments in a speech. This information should make an impact, so be sure it does. Keep in mind that information alone generally will not sway your audience; how you present it will. Images and reading are great ways to break up the spoken word and draw your audience in.

A Closer Look at Stories and Examples – CPR for Your Presentations

My daughter is famous for her "Drew and Austin" stories; they're a highlight at family gatherings. If anyone new joins us, it's generally a good excuse to pull out the stops, let the stories fly, and laugh till we cry.

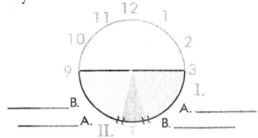

98

This is because stories are powerful. They can shift a mood, open a heart, or change a perspective. They immediately pull your audience in, make you more real and conversational, and set the table for the rest of the course to come. The fact is, they remain with the audience long after the presentation ends and far longer than the main points.

It's interesting to look at memory and retrieval with respect to storytelling. We generally remember the story first and then work backward to other aspects of a presentation. A memory trail is a pathway of sorts used by our brains to recall information. Images and stories stimulate more senses, allowing for more pathways back to the presentation. Most listeners quickly forget the main points, but images, readings, and stories function like portals, taking us back into the experience, which triggers the memory backwards to the key ideas of a presentation.

Many people who don't speak for a living – most of us, in other words – spend way too much time deciding what our main points are and too little time finding examples and stories to make them memorable and convincing. If your main points make sense to your audience, the next most important thing to do is reinforce them with memorable supporting material in the form of stories and examples.

Also remember that well-rounded presentations appeal to both logical and emotional audience members. After all, audiences are always made up of a little bit of both. Some people are more tuned in to the facts (logical), whereas others want to know the impact (emotional).

When presenting numbers, remember that they too tell a story. What is the story behind those numbers? Why does this group need to know this story? How will it help your audience make a decision?

Flip "I'm Not a Good Storyteller" on Its Ear

There's only one way to get beyond that statement: start telling more stories. Go to lunch and tell a co-worker or friend something that happened this past weekend. Make notes of funny moments or experiences that rocked your world. Then work backward. What are the real nuggets of the story? Why did it strike you as funny or stupid, sad or ironic?

The more you tell stories, the easier it is for you to hear them as you say them. You will begin to notice subtleties such as rhythm and timing.

Pick a handful of stories and begin working them into conversations. With conscious effort and awareness, you can become a good storyteller even if you don't start off that way.

Develop Some Go-to Stories

Most of us are asked to speak about the company or industry we represent, the volunteer work we do, or a personal experience that others can learn from, such as travel. For these occasions, it's extremely helpful to have a handful of go-to stories. These are stories you know inside and out and can apply to a wide range of audiences. The beauty of these stories is that they can expand or contract depending on the audience; this makes them ideal for moments when you did not expect to be speaking.

Find stories that best convey something human about your industry. Find stories that bring to life your company's value statement and/or your volunteer work. I.e., why do you work for this group? What moves you about their mission statement, and when have you seen it in action? Tell these stories.

How Many Stories?

When preparing your presentation, be sure to include at least two stories for each main point. The more time you have to speak, the more stories and examples you can use.

If you have three main points, you should prepare six stories or examples. If you're speaking for more than twenty-five minutes, you probably have time to add more depth to each of your three main points. The longer you have to speak, the greater your opportunity to involve your audience.

Asking and answering questions, playing videos, showing vivid pictures, readings, demonstrations, funny stuff...These are all great elements to add.

Editing during Your Presentation

Earlier in this chapter, I talked about time management. What part of the presentation can you edit during an actual presentation? You can't edit the main points because you previewed them and your audience knows you're going to talk about them. What your audience does not know is exactly what you're going to say about each main point. They don't know your stories and examples, so you can edit, or prune, these. In so doing, you can manage your time.

If, for example, you're running short on time and haven't yet touched on your third main point, cut one of your stories from main point two and move on to your third main point.

If you're still short on time, share only one story in main point three.

Another time you may want to edit is when your first story was a smashing success, one you hit out of the proverbial ballpark. If this story was exceptionally strong, move on. If your first story was good but didn't completely hit the mark, tell the second story.

Transitions

Transitions are bridges between main ideas. They play an organizing role in your speech. They link one main point to the next and keep the presentation moving in a forward direction.

An effective transition consists of one clean sentence that sounds like this: "Now that I've talked about the myth of credit, I want to focus on the freedom of being debt free."

With two main points, use one transition. With three main points, use two transitions.

2 Main Points

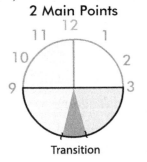

Transition

3 Main Points

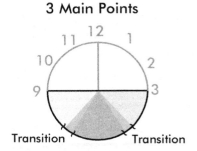

Transition   Transition

The key with transitions is to remember to keep them clear and short. Always use the same words when transitioning that you used when you previewed the main points. In the example above, I used the exact same wording as earlier – "myth of credit" and "debt free" – so as not to confuse my audience by switching things up.

In essence, the transition provides a clean-up moment. Because audience members drift and daydream, transitions are opportunities for them to jump back in.

Chapter Summary

The body is the meat; it's why people come to listen to you. Be sure to respect your audience by narrowing your main points down to only two or three. Choose your main points and your stories based on who you're speaking to, and remember that stories and examples perform CPR on your main points by breathing life into your ideas.

Chapter Twelve:

Own It

Courage stood alone, in front, and was good with it.
- Onlee Bowden

I n the end, public speaking always boils down to the very real fact that when you speak in front of others, there you are! Are you as ready as you could be? It's time to find out. Let's take what you've been learning and try it on for size.

Create Your Own Presentation

It's now time to put it all together and create your own presentations. It's common to want to jump in with an upcoming presentation in your field of expertise, but I'd prefer that you begin a little before that. Why? Because your brain will be more relaxed when nothing is on the line, which means you will learn faster.

Below are three presentation topics, each designed to help you become more fluent with structure. Using the Bowden Speaking Wheel, create a presentation for each of these topics. (Remember, your topic is also called the "big idea.")

Topic One: Advice to Grandchildren

We all have one thing in common: we had grandparents. We didn't all know our grandparents, nor were all grandparents good role models, but if we live long enough, we might be lucky enough to have children who look to us for guidance and understanding.

Take a few minutes and capture what you would want to say to your grandchildren. Make a list of ideas in no particular order. From this list, choose three that stand out to you as your main points. In this case, three pieces of advice to grandchildren are your three main points. What stories will you use to bring your main points to life? Pick them.

Now continue to develop your presentation by filling in the introduction and conclusion, and remember to start your presentation with a story.

Topic Two: If You Were Debt Free, How Would This Change You?

"Debt free" is fast becoming an obsolete notion in our society, as many people only associate it with "over 70" retirement plans. Believe it or not, living in debt is simply a paradigm we choose to believe in.

My grandparents never had debt, and my parents very little. In the 1980s, things changed. Within less than a decade, debt became part of achieving the American dream. Credit now equals access to a more coveted lifestyle, yet are we really free?

It's been said that debt enslaves us to the debtor. Just in case there's any truth to this, let's consider life without debt. Enjoy the topic.

Topic Three: If I Were in Charge...

Who doesn't want to be in charge at some point? I tell my clients to simply look at whatever is really bugging them right now and take charge of it. For this one presentation, the world is your oyster, and you get to form the pearl.

Usually, open-ended topics require two brainstorming sessions. First, brainstorm what you want to be in charge of, then brainstorm your three main points as well as your supporting stories and examples.

These are excellent first presentation topics to help develop your understanding of structure building, creativity, and finding stories and examples. If you treat these topics like a game and figure out how to fill in the blanks on the speaking wheel, you will be more prepared when it's time to speak in the real world on your own topics.

Consider Scheduling an Online Consultation Session

Once you've taken my course or read this book and developed these three topics into presentations, consider working individually with me, face to face.

Each on-line session is fifty minutes in length and is designed to give you real practice without the extra costs of travel or time away from work. I will offer feedback on your speaking wheel, help you fine-tune your stories, and provide feedback on your delivery.

These sessions are supplemental to the course and reading material and are a separate charge. Please visit the course home page at for more information.

Chapter Summary

From now until the end, speak your thoughts, share your ideas, and stand up for those who cannot. Decide now to toast your son's graduation, speak at the next conference, or simply share a thought at the next meeting.

It's time to own it.

Appendix:

The Bowden Speaking Wheel and Presenter Patty Cantrell, TEDx Talks, Manhattan

In Flip It on Its Ear, I deconstructed public speaking to help you gain a greater understanding of the skill sets utilized while speaking effectively. The question now is what does effective public speaking look like when all these skills are put back together?

To find out, I'd like you to watch a TEDx Manhattan presentation given by Patty Cantrell in 2012. Patty was a client of mine, and we worked on several presentations during a three-year period.

As I mentioned earlier, Patty is a brilliant writer and much sought-after speaker, and her presentation on the topic of sustainable agriculture is an excellent example of using the Bowden Speaking Wheel.

I would like you to pay special attention to her use of structure via the wheel plus her stance, use of PowerPoint, storytelling, and how she stays inside the speaking triangle yet has great energy. Look at how she uses a story to begin and additional examples from other industries to drive home her message. Is she dealing with being nervous? Sure she is! This presentation is in the big leagues, and she really gets it right.

I was delighted when Patty gave me permission to use her presentation in this course, and I want to encourage you to watch it a few times, maybe more than a few times, to get more familiar with the structure she uses, from her attention getter to how she states the big idea to her preview. Notice how warm and welcoming she is, how down to earth, how effective.

They say that imitation is the sincerest form of flattery. Get to work and do some serious imitating!

For more information about courses, to view presentations, or to download The Bowden Speaking Wheel please go to www. FlipItOnItsEar.com

Author Biography

Onlee Bowden

Teacher, author, professional speaker, communication strategist

In 1985, Onlee received her master's degree from Central Michigan University in organizational and public communication. She remained on CMU's faculty until the early 1990s teaching courses in advanced public speaking, leadership, organizational communication, and teamwork. She left CMU to begin her own consulting firm, where she specialized in professional speech coaching, organizational development, and executive consulting. As a communication specialist, she followed the 1992 presidential campaigns and was a regular guest in George Weeks' Detroit News Sunday column.

In 2008, Onlee authored Another Great Story, a Grand Traverse Chamber of Commerce book that tells the back stories of thirty-seven entrepreneurs who live and work in the Grand Traverse area.

Onlee's professional roles include vice president of organizational development for the Grand Traverse Resort, president of training and development for Horizon Enterprises, Inc., director of marketing and public relations for Traverse City State Bank, and owner of

Onlee Bowden LLC, In Your Own Words, Training and Professional Development.

Included in Onlee's client list are former Alma Mayor Nancy Gallagher, The Honorable Judge Jack Arnold of Gratiot County, National Geographic Adventure Journalist Tom Clynes, 2008 Small Business of the Year recipient Terry Umlor of Springfield Roofing, Traverse City Area Chamber of Commerce President Douglas Luciani, and TedX Manhattan presenter Patty Cantrell.

Her passion work involves living in a small mountain village in Haiti, where she teaches adults and children about the power of creativity and imagination.

Onlee, her husband Lee Torrey, and their two dogs Finn and Bea work and play in Traverse City, MI, a northern Michigan destination gem.

CPSIA information can be obtained
at www.ICGtesting.com
Printed in the USA
BVOW06s1951041017
496758BV00009B/55/P